IT HAPPENED IN WISCONSIN

IT HAPPENED IN
WISCONSIN

Michael Bie

TWODOT®

GUILFORD, CONNECTICUT
HELENA, MONTANA

AN IMPRINT OF THE GLOBE PEQUOT PRESS

A · **T W O D O T**® · **B O O K**

Copyright © 2007 Morris Book Publishing, LLC

Front cover photo: Wooden arches for Howard Morey Airplane Hangar, Jonesville. Library of Congress, LC-USZ62-95940.
Back cover photo: A morning's catch in Oconomowoc. Library of Congress, LC-USZ62-102332.
Text design by Nancy Freeborn
Map by M. A. Dubé © 2007 Morris Book Publishing, LLC

Library of Congress Cataloging-in-Publication Data
Bie, Mike.
  It happened in Wisconsin/Michael Bie.—1st ed.
     p. cm.—(It happened in series)
  Includes bibliographical references and index.
  ISBN-13: 978-0-7627-4153-3
  ISBN-10: 0-7627-4153-8
  1. Wisconsin—History—Anecdotes. 2. Wisconsin—Biography—Anecdotes. I. Title.
  F581.6.B54 2007
  977.5—dc22

                                                                        2006038422

Manufactured in the United States of America
First Edition/Second Printing

CONTENTS

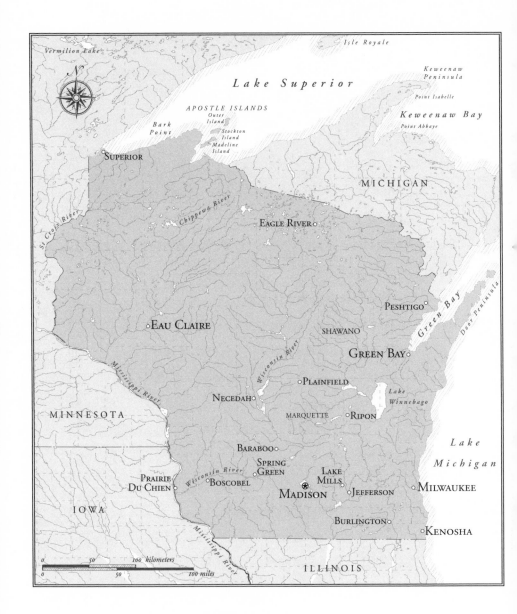

WISCONSIN

CONTENTS

INTRODUCTION

When a man named Henry Abel made the long trek from Philadelphia in 1838 to conduct a survey of the Wisconsin Territory, he was aiming to compile a report for emigrants, travelers, and local residents about the "new but rapidly improving portion of the great West." It was to be a kind of early travel guide, minus the restaurant reviews. Abel noted the climate, the major rivers and lakes, the common flora and fauna, a few "curiosities," and even the handful of newspapers found in the territory. Summing up, he said, "These are the gardens of the West."

Abel was most likely referring to Wisconsin's landscape, but he could have just as well been alluding to the territory's potential for cultivating a bounty of compelling stories. These homegrown tales have come from the likes of progressive Bob La Follette and regressive Joe McCarthy, circus pioneer Al Ringling and circus-from-hell master Ed Gein.

Wisconsin has produced champion cheese and bathtub beer, a major political party and a self-proclaimed "king." From the Badger State also came Earth Day and the bombing of Sterling Hall, both in the same year. Lurking in the shadows were Jeffrey Dahmer, John Dillinger, and a would-be assassin nobody remembers.

The state agitated famously for the abolition of slavery and watched helplessly the rise of racist paramilitary sects 125 years later.

We welcomed a young baseball icon and shot the dog of a Green Bay Packer head coach.

It Happened In Wisconsin tells these stories and more, thirty in all, ranging in time from 3000 BC to AD 1991. As you have probably gathered, this is not a textbook. The monumental events in Wisconsin history are included here, but *It Happened In Wisconsin* is the first modern collection I know that includes the famous and the obscure, the inspirational and the tragic, the important and the just plain weird. In short, the things that make Wisconsin, Wisconsin. And I was hard-pressed to stop at thirty. The state has been endowed with stunning natural resources, a colorful cast of characters, and scores of remarkable happenings. If somebody were looking to confirm all the stereotypes about the boring Midwest, they would have to look elsewhere—Illinois, perhaps.

I'm fifth-generation, and I'm lucky to have spent years traipsing through the state to write about the things that make Wisconsin unique. (I personally witnessed one of the events in this book, but I won't replay that now.) Whether you are an emigrant, traveler, or resident, I hope you enjoy these thirty true stories from the garden of the West.

AZTALAN: BONES OF CONTENTION

- 3000 BC -

WHEN THE WILSON BROTHERS PUT THEIR BOAT IN Rock Lake for a day
of duck hunting, they had no idea they would be stirring up a mystery dating back thousands of years—a mystery that lingers yet today.

Rock Lake, located near the community of Lake Mills in south
central Wisconsin, was unusually clear that day in 1900 when the
brothers ventured out, shotguns in hand. A lack of rain had dropped
the water level, and as they paddled their skiff across the lake, the
Wilsons noticed something strange below the surface. It looked like
rocks stacked neatly in the shape of a pyramid.

Back in town, word spread quickly about the discovery. Indian
legends about "rock teepees" built by mysterious ancient people were
well known to locals. Dozens of residents took to their boats. Some
dove into the water to touch the formation, described as a tent-
shaped structure about one hundred feet long.

Within days the lake silt was up to its usual tricks. Water clarity
dimmed and the structure disappeared into the watery depths once

again, taking with it proof positive that there was some truth behind the legends.

In the coming decades, aerial sightings were made of the Rock Lake "pyramid." When a local teacher recruited members of the University of Wisconsin swim team to dive on the site, their confirmation of a rock structure drew considerable attention from the press. It also drew the attention of the state archaeological office, which conducted its own dive and found nothing. The authorities declared fraud and the teacher was forced to resign his job.

In 1937 a famous diver named Max Nohl found another tall, cone-shaped pyramid on the south end of the lake, but the strange pyramids of Rock Lake were forgotten again until 1967, when a skin diver found a structure about one hundred feet long and twenty feet high on the murky bottom. His discovery was published in a diving magazine.

Yet again the pyramids were forgotten until a diving team, this time using sonar technology, located the structures and the first images were recorded. That was 1991.

Ongoing research has yielded the identification of at least five artificial structures in Rock Lake. Experts hesitate to date the constructions—which are made of fitted, stacked rocks—but one prevailing theory suggests they were built by prehistoric copper cultures three thousand years ago.

One thing is certain: the area is rife with mysteries generated from the remains of a lost civilization known as Aztalan, Wisconsin's premier archaeological site located just a few miles from Rock Lake. A marker at Aztalan State Park attempts to accomplish in one paragraph what archaeologists have filled volumes trying to explain:

Indians of more advanced culture than surrounding
tribes occupied a village on this site around the year

1500. They were strangers to this region and their cannibalism made them unsatisfactory neighbors. The strength of their stockade walls proves they lived in a hostile world. The original village had a population of about 500. The area enclosed by the stockade contained about 21 acres and within the stockade were cornfields as well as houses and temples.

Eventually the village was destroyed by other local Indian tribes, leaving no known survivors of the Aztalan people.

Whoa there. Just one second, professor. What was that?

"Their cannibalism made them unsatisfactory neighbors."

Well, we guess so. Cannibalism rates somewhat worse than borrowing your neighbor's snow blower and returning it in the spring with an empty gas tank.

Modern studies link Aztalan to the Mississippian Indian civilization, which flourished along its namesake river region from Wisconsin to the Gulf Coast. Sometime around 1100 AD, a group of Mississippians migrated north to the Crawfish River in southern Wisconsin. They lived there for roughly 150 years before mysteriously disappearing from the Midwest, leaving behind tens of thousands of artifacts and more than a few unanswered questions.

Samuel Barrett, the first anthropologist to work in the state, spent two years digging at Aztalan in 1919 and 1920, publishing his findings in a book considered the definitive work on Aztalan archaeology. The book focuses on the walls and small houses that once existed on the site. He also discovered the elaborate burial site of a young woman who was wrapped in thousands of beads.

Barrett's findings went from academic to sensational when he concluded that the people of Aztalan were cannibals. "Barrett based this extraordinary claim," wrote contemporary Aztalan experts Robert Birmingham and Lynne Goldstein, "on his discovery of many hundreds of butchered, broken, and burned human bones in refuse areas; severed limbs in fire pits; and discarded skulls, including one that clearly had been cut from the torso."

The early excavations unearthed a surprising number of human bones showing clear signs of cutting and dismemberment. Some had been opened to extract marrow, a practice normally reserved for animal bones.

Paul Parmalee, an expert on animal food remains, wrote in 1960 that there was evidence some human bones had been processed like animal bones—while noting that the community's major source of protein had come from deer, fish, and other animals.

In their 2005 book, *Aztalan: Mysteries of an Ancient Indian Town*, Birmingham and Goldstein refute the cannibalism theory unequivocally. "Early twentieth-century researchers erroneously described the ancient people as cannibals who used their neighbors as food." Cannibalism "remained part of the official interpretation for many years because the behavior represented by the remains was so different from anything archaeologists had seen to date."

The current line maintains that some of the people here had been victims of "violent customs associated with intense warfare," including the taking of trophy heads and other body parts, the torture and mutilation of prisoners, and last—but certainly not least—the consumption of body parts as *ritual.* These rituals were part of well-documented funerary customs of the Mississippian culture.

While it's not as unsettling as having had true cannibals living in the backyard, the talk of trophy heads, body parts, torture, and ritualistic taste-testing ranks fairly high on the ick scale.

"What is so unusual about Aztalan compared to other period sites, however, is that so much fragmentary broken and cut human bone was discarded," according to Birmingham and Goldstein. "Indeed, while much has been learned about this spectacular site over the years, many great questions remain."

Why did the Mississippians come here in the first place? Where did they go, and why? And what about those pyramids in Rock Lake?

Prevailing wisdom goes that ancient peoples—earlier than the Mississippians, perhaps as early as 3000 BC—had built rock pyramids and tombs for their dead near a small lake. This would coincide with the low lake levels of the time.

Pioneers coming to the area in the 1830s discovered the Aztalan ruins and heard Winnebago Indian legends of a sacred site in the lake. Postglacial activity apparently had filled the lake, and the structures were submerged—except for strange protrusions just above the water. When sawmills dammed up the flowage of Rock Lake, the water levels rose significantly, and the structures disappeared far below the surface.

That is, until two duck hunters began to stir up the mysteries of Rock Lake.

LOST AND FOUND

- 1634 -

FRENCH EXPLORER JEAN NICOLET WAS LOST. Really lost. Half-a-world lost.

Wearing a full-length silk robe and firing pistols to announce his arrival, at least he had style on that summer afternoon in 1634 when he stepped out of his canoe to ask for directions.

Only fourteen years after the pilgrims landed on the Atlantic Coast, Nicolet advanced seven hundred miles west through the Straits of Mackinac, across Lake Michigan, around the tip of the peninsula separating the great lake, and into Green Bay.

"He wore a grand robe of China damask, all strewn with flowers and birds of many colors," wrote a contemporary, missionary Barthelemy Vimont. "No sooner did they perceive him than the women and children fled, at the sight of a man who carried thunder in both hands—for thus they called the two pistols that he held. The news of his coming quickly spread to the places round about, and there assembled four or five thousand men. Each of the chief men made a feast for him, and at one of these banquets they served at least six score beavers."

The local Winnebago Indians who greeted Nicolet on the shores of Green Bay were bewildered, but they welcomed the stranger and served him dinner. In the back of Nicolet's mind, however, had to be the untimely fate of one of his colleagues, Etienne Brule, who had died at the hands of the Huron Indians a year earlier. Brule and the Hurons had been on good terms. Such was life for the intrepid men like Nicolet who "discovered" the Great Lakes region in the 1600s. Constantly attacked by mosquitoes (if not the locals), surviving treacherous swells on open water, fending off starvation, all this and more was in a day's work.

That's why Samuel de Champlain, an experienced explorer in his own right (Lake Champlain is his namesake), established a network of adventurous young men to move farther west into the Great Lakes region and claim lands for God and France. Champlain's first protégé was Etienne Brule.

The most important thing about the exploration business, Champlain tutored his men, was adapting to the ways of the native inhabitants.

You could say that Brule embraced this idea, particularly in regard to the Indian maidens.

Brule was something of a rock star in his day, but like most celebrities who forget their roots, he crashed and burned. Champlain, who had affectionately called Brule "my lad," would eventually denounce him as a young man "without religion," prone to "unrestrained debauchery and libertinism" with the natives. The other explorers, Jesuit missionaries especially, loathed him.

In 1629 when the English attacked Quebec (the French colony settled by Champlain), Brule betrayed his nation by collaborating with the enemy. When England was defeated, Brule fled into the wilderness to live with the Huron Indians.

Justice was served for Brule. In fact, justice was a serving of Brule. He met his end when the Hurons, for reasons we can only imagine, clubbed him to death and ate him. Talk about French cuisine.

Jean Nicolet was the anti-Brule, a workmanlike explorer and interpreter who was highly respected by his peers. He kept his hands off the native women.

With Brule out of the starting lineup for good, Champlain tapped Nicolet, a loyal servant of New France and all-around good guy, to establish friendly relations with the "people of the sea."

What Champlain meant by "people of the sea" is subject to some debate. We know Champlain hoped to find a route to China. Did he believe the "people of the sea" were Chinese?

In light of Nicolet donning a dashing Chinese robe when he arrived at Green Bay, conventional wisdom has assumed that the explorer believed he was stepping ashore in China. It's been the cornerstone of every fourth-grade Wisconsin history class since who knows when.

Some scholars, however, have come to dispute the long-accepted notion that Jean Nicolet believed he had reached China.

"There is no direct evidence that Nicolet was seeking contact with Asia," wrote Jerrold Rodesch, a history professor at the University of Wisconsin–Green Bay.

> The "grand robe of China damask, all strewn with
> flowers and birds of many colors" he wore would have
> been, along with his thundering pistols, impressive
> enough to establish his claims to special authority even
> if he were merely meeting with the Winnebago on the
> peace mission for which a record exists. There is no
> particular logic in an attempt to disguise himself as
> Chinese. The Asian connection like so much else in the
> story is speculative and inferential. And also plausible.
> We know the French sought a route to Asia. We know

Champlain, who commissioned Nicolet's service, was
especially hopeful about finding a way to Asia.

Maybe Nicolet thought he had reached China, maybe not. Like the question of whether Brule was the first white man to "discover" our land, we'll never know for sure.

The one thing we do know is that Jean Nicolet landed in Green Bay in 1634 and enjoyed barbecued beavers with his friendly hosts. A statue of Nicolet stands near the presumed spot of his arrival.

"Champlain, always anxious to promote the expansion of New France, must have been disappointed over the outcome of Nicolet's journey," wrote Alice Smith in *The History of Wisconsin, Volume I.* "True, Nicolet had made new friends for the French, but he had found only more Indians, and the sea upon which their country bordered was not the Pacific, not the Gulf of Mexico, and not the Gulf of California; nor was any route to the ocean opened up on the voyage."

Not helping matters is the fact that Nicolet's notes were lost during his time, and Nicolet himself was lost to history for a long, long time.

Starting in 1632 all French explorers and Jesuit missionaries submitted their journals for publication. In 1673 the annual publications stopped, and copies became extremely rare. Not until 1858 did the Canadian government reprint the entire series. An English translation wasn't completed until 1903, 296 years after Nicolet's journey!

Although Nicolet's journal was lost, repeated references by his contemporaries spoke highly of the man, and an account of Nicolet's passage to find the "people of the sea" was detailed by Father Vimont in 1642.

Vimont's account was written as a eulogy. En route to Quebec on a mercy mission for an Indian captive, Nicolet's boat capsized in a sudden swell.

It sure wasn't easy discovering a new world.

PASSION IN PRAIRIE DU CHIEN

- 1832 -

IT DIDN'T TAKE LONG FOR THE YOUNG LOVERS TO devise a way to see each other. Since Jeff was forbidden to visit Sarah at her home on the fort grounds, the young woman would tell her parents she was taking her little brother and sisters for a walk along the Mississippi. Once clear of the compound, along the sun-splashed banks of the river, Sarah would happen to run into Jeff, the dashing young lieutenant and West Point graduate.

The children were allowed to play at a safe distance from the couple, and Jeff and Sarah finally had time alone under the willows and oaks, where nature took its course as surely as the river flowed to the sea. In due time, the couple became engaged, even though Jeff had the misfortune of serving under Sarah's disapproving father, the company commander. The couple braced for his inevitable response.

"I'll be damned if another daughter of mine will marry into the army!"

The father who only wanted the best for his daughter was

Colonel Zachary Taylor, commandant of Fort Crawford in Prairie du Chien in the 1830s, and later the nation's twelfth president.

His daughter, Sarah Knox Taylor, "Knoxie," only wanted to be with the love of her life, Lieutenant Jefferson Davis, who was destined to serve as the president of the Confederate States of America.

Small world, eh?

Problem was, as daughters of a career military man living in a godforsaken wilderness outpost, the Taylor girls had but two choices: date a soldier or don't date at all. The old man had pretty much eliminated the first option.

"Knowing the hardships of a military wife," reads the official White House history, "Taylor opposed his daughters' marrying career soldiers."

A case could be made that Zachary Taylor didn't even want Jeff Davis *looking* at his daughter. Davis was ordered time and time again for duty far from Prairie du Chien. He was sent off logging in northern Wisconsin, busting squatters in Illinois (they almost killed him in a mine shaft), and pursing defiant Indians throughout the territory.

When Davis *was* in Prairie du Chien—"prairie of the dog," as named by French fur traders—Colonel Taylor insisted on being present at all fort socials when the lovebirds might have an opportunity to mingle. Imagine having the man known as "Ol' Rough & Ready" giving you the evil eye at the Friday night mixer.

"It's time for all honest people to be in bed," Taylor would bark at Davis in announcing the party was over.

Taylor claimed to have the "kindliest feelings" for Davis, but things were tenuous between the two men, and when Davis sided against his commander on a minor point of order during a court-martial case, well, Davis found himself "promoted" to the Southwest Territory.

But time and distance could not extinguish the flames of passion begun in Prairie du Chien.

This nugget comes from Davis's papers, written December 19, 1834:

> *[Your] kind, dear letter, I have kissed it often and it*
> *has driven many mad notions from my brain. Sarah*
> *whatever I may be hereafter I will ascribe to you.*
> *Neglected by you I should be worse than nothing and if*
> *the few good qualities I possess shall under your smiles*
> *yield a fruit it will be yours as the grain is the hus-*
> *bandman's. . . . Shall we not soon meet Sarah to part*
> *no more? Oh! how I long to lay my head upon that*
> *breast which beats in unison with my own, to turn*
> *from the sickening sights of worldly duplicity and look*
> *in those eyes so eloquent of purity and love.*

Obviously the guy had it bad for young Sarah. That's probably why he resigned his commission in 1835. Finally realizing that the starry-eyed couple would do what they wanted, Colonel Taylor consented to the marriage.

The new couple moved to Mississippi to start their life together on a small plantation. In a sentimental letter to Prairie du Chien, Sarah said she imagined her mother skimming milk in the cellar or feeding the chickens.

Within three months of her wedding, Sarah was dead from malaria. Davis mourned for years. He didn't remarry for a decade.

Thirteen years after Sarah's death, in 1848, Davis was given command of a regiment of Mississippians in the Mexican War. He served with distinction under, you guessed it, his former father-in-law. The men, each carrying long-held sorrow over Sarah's death, reconciled their relationship.

But before long, politics intervened. Following the war, Taylor was elected president and Davis was appointed to the United States Senate. Even though he was the owner of one hundred slaves, Taylor, ever the dutiful military man, vehemently opposed secession. He hadn't risked his neck all those years in the military to see the Union break apart. In a White House meeting, Taylor told fellow Southerners he would hang secessionists "with less reluctance than he had hanged deserters and spies in Mexico."

Davis, of course, went on to become the one and only president of the ill-fated Confederacy. One of his generals was Richard Taylor, "little Dickie" as he was known in the Prairie du Chien days. The younger brother of Sarah, Richard was one of the child witnesses to her romantic liaisons along the Mississippi. He was also Zachary Taylor's only son.

End of story, right?

Not quite. For decades afterward it was widely accepted in Wisconsin that young Jeff Davis was something less than an officer and a gentleman.

In a pioneer retrospective written in 1895, the Honorable Joseph T. Mills tells of his early days tutoring the Taylor children at Fort Crawford. "The heartbroken father," Mills said of Taylor, "knew Davis as a professional libertine, unprincipled and incapable of sincere affection for Knox unless he coveted the money to which she was heir."

Ouch.

The Taylors, he continued, "were reticent and lonely as if oppressed by some deep family secret, not to be disclosed to a stranger."

Then Mills drops the bomb.

"Anthropologists have traced Jefferson Davis' descendants among the papooses that some years since rolled, laughed and tumbled on the mats of some doting Winnebago, Sioux or Chippewa matron, of whom she is now proud, for she has enriched and diversified posterity by the new and noisy tribe of Davis."

The story persisted a hundred years after Davis was stationed in Wisconsin. In 1933, the *Shawano Leader-Advocate* ran a story about the death of the last-known Civil War veteran in the area, a member of the Menominee Indian tribe.

"He had the unique distinction of being the son of Jefferson Davis, the father of the Southern Confederacy," the article states. "This fact while being known by several persons on the reservation and by several old-time residents of this community, has sometimes been disputed, but there are enough people acquainted with the facts to prove conclusively that he was indeed the son of the southerner."

Short of a DNA test, history will never know for sure. While it's clear that Zachary Taylor didn't want his daughters marrying into the military, could it be that the "deep family secret" cited by Mills contributed to those early misgivings over Taylor's beloved Knoxie marrying a man with morals as loose as Jefferson Davis?

KING JAMES STRANG

- 1844 -

JAMES STRANG—PROPHET, SEER, AND TRANSLATOR (appointed by God, no less)— strode along the White River near Burlington, four apostles at his heels. Strang possessed a gift for language that had converted any number of skeptics but his attention was focused now on this small group that were already believers as the group made its way along the Edenic setting by the river. He was in the midst of revealing a message from God, and his followers clung to his every word.

The revelation, Strang explained, had told him that the records of an ancient people were buried nearby on a small hill, "The Hill of Promise."

"Unto thee it is reserved," Strang quoted God. "Take heed that thou count it not a light thing . . . as thou servest me faithfully and comest not short, thou shalt unlock the mysteries thereof, which I have kept hid from the world."

He led the men to an oak tree on a hill. Three feet under the tree they would find a case containing the records. Strang told his apostles to examine the ground closely to make sure they were not being "imposed upon."

"We examined as we dug all the way with the utmost care," wrote the followers, "and we say, with utmost confidence, that no part of the earth through which we dug exhibited any sign or indication that it had been moved or disturbed at any time previous."

Sure enough, three feet down the men found a case. Inside were three brass plates inscribed with a mysterious language. Only he could interpret the plates, Strang told the wide-eyed, slack-jawed apostles.

James J. Strang had arrived in Burlington in 1843 equipped with two highly dangerous things: a magnetic personality and a law degree. "I am eager and mankind is frail," he had written in his diary as a young man. "I shall act upon it in time to come for my own benefit."

After settling in Burlington, he made a quick jaunt down to Nauvoo, Illinois, where he won over Mormon founder Joseph Smith. Strang was baptized by Smith and was made a church elder in a matter of weeks. He was then given the mission of building a Mormon community in Wisconsin.

Armed with the brass plates as proof of his divine visions, Strang returned to Burlington, which became "the site of one of the weirdest colonizing schemes ever attempted," according to a historian who interviewed the last surviving colonist in the 1920s. Strang's kingdom, Voree—"Garden of Peace"—was located two miles west of Burlington on the White River. It thrived, growing to about two thousand members and even publishing a newspaper.

Strang's frequent "revelations" from God usually went like this: "Therefore, my servant James, if thou wilt receive honor and glory, verily, verily, thou shalt lead my people, and in my word shalt thou receive from me and teach unto my people."

With his authority in place, Strang's revelations went heavy on enforcement: "With words of fire shalt thou consume those whose voices are raised against thee, and their hearts shall fail them at thy rebuke, until they are altogether cast off, and my Spirit departs from them."

The first sign that something was rotten in the garden came when Joseph Smith was murdered in Nauvoo and Strang claimed he was heir apparent to lead the Mormon Church, producing a letter signed by Smith that stated as much. The document, however, was deemed a forgery and a council headed by Brigham Young declared Strang a fraud. A couple of years later, Young led the flock to Utah— the best thing that had ever happened to Strang, who was now unencumbered by church oversight.

Like any despot, Strang soon began consolidating his grip. Coincidentally, God kept giving him instructions to purge those who expressed dissent. A man holding the title of one of the first presidents of the church was the first to go. One of Strang's counselors went next.

Then Strang had another vision, and this one included him taking multiple wives and living on Lake Michigan's Beaver Island. Once there, Strang crowned himself "King of the Kingdom of God on Earth" and the woohoohoo was on.

Strang set the bar for generations of cults to come.

The king's coronation was a sight, "one of the most spectacular impositions ever practiced before deluded American citizens," according to the *Green Bay Advocate*. Strang wore a tin crown and a robe lifted from a Shakespearean actor.

Every subject was made to contribute 10 percent of his or her income to the kingdom, not an onerous requirement but one enforced under threat of a visit to the whipping post. Nonsubjects, the several hundred fishermen and lumberjacks on the island, were required to contribute as well, under the same threat.

Strang soon opened up a mint and began printing his own island currency. All official positions, including sheriff and police deputies, were made by the king's appointment. Opponents had a tendency to turn up missing from the island. A cannon was purchased to "protect" against invaders.

The guy had everything but the Kool-Aid.

Strang mandated that all church elders have a minimum of two wives. He followed his own decree with gusto, taking five wives and fathering twelve children.

But like any tyrant worth his salt, Strang eventually went too far. He outlawed coffee, tea, tobacco, and booze on the island, and then indulged his peculiar obsession for women in trousers. "He decreed that the female portion of the island should wear a hideous costume of calico pantalets," according to an eyewitness account in the *Green Bay Advocate*. "This garment came to the ankle and was not unlike Turkish trousers. Over it was worn one flimsy skirt that reached to the knee. Beads, jewelry, and all personal adornment were tabooed. According to the decree of the king the hair was 'slicked' back and braided tightly."

Women with curly hair had to tame their disobedient locks with bear oil.

One female subject refused to wear the required pants, and as punishment her husband was taken to the streets and whipped.

The fishermen and lumberjacks who worked on or around the island weren't happy with this state of affairs either. In one instance, when a group of outsiders demanded the sale of whiskey at the island trading post, Strang's followers fired a cannon into the crowd.

Trouble in paradise reached a boiling point in the summer of 1856. The man who had been whipped for his wife's disobedience of the dress code, along with an accomplice, caught Strang unaware one day and shot the king at point-blank range. The gunmen then pistol-whipped Strang until one of the guns broke. Mortally wounded, Strang lingered, comforted by Betsey and Phoebe, two of his teenage wives. He asked to be returned to his artificial kingdom, Voree, to die. His wish was their command. He died on July 9—leaving behind five wives, four of whom were pregnant.

The weird kingdom of Voree ended with a gunshot, as weird kingdoms often do. A simple tombstone in the Burlington cemetery says nothing about the man who was its king, James Strang. Not enough tablet space to mention LOVING HUSBAND OF MARY, BETSEY, PHOEBE, ELVIRA, AND SARAH.

JOHN McCAFFARY'S BODY

- 1851 -

KENOSHA WAS ON EDGE. It had been a hot summer, with the stench of cesspools, animal waste, and rotting garbage filling the air, and now in the waning days of July, a cholera epidemic was sweeping the city.

John and Bridgett McCaffary (sometimes spelled "McCaffrey"), cooped up in their house like everyone else, began to argue. Their marriage had not been a model of domestic bliss. The boarders who lived upstairs heard the couple argue all the time. On occasion the sounds of crockery smashing against the walls carried through the neighborhood.

It was a hot July night in 1850 and the McCaffarys were at it again. Their argument moved into the dim backyard where the neighbors—the Daleys, Mitchells, and Gridleys, among others—could clearly hear the yelling. Then Bridgett began to scream: "John, spare me! No, John! Save me!"

The hotheaded Irishman tightened his grip on Bridgett's neck and dragged her, flailing, to a corner of the yard, where he upended her headfirst into a water barrel. He held her down until the trembling stopped.

Bridgett McCaffary drowned in eighteen inches of watery crud.

Neighbors arrived to see John climbing out of the large "hogshead" barrel. One of them asked if his wife was inside the barrel.

Well, ah, er, *somebody* was inside, he replied.

Not the sharpest tool in the shed, that John McCaffary.

Capital punishment had been an accepted practice while Wisconsin was still part of the Michigan Territory (1818–1836) and at least five executions had taken place during Wisconsin's territorial days (1836–1848). The possibility of execution as punishment was still on the books in May 1851, three years after statehood, when McCaffary was pronounced guilty of murder after ninety minutes of jury deliberation.

"I am now about to perform by far the most painful act of my judicial life," Judge E. V. Whiton told the packed courtroom as he began sentencing the first person to be executed in the new state of Wisconsin. "By our law, the crime of which you stand convicted is the only one that is punishable with death."

Whiton summarized the overwhelming evidence against McCaffary and then, as if to convince himself that the death penalty was justified, Whiton detailed the "peculiar atrocity" that made the crime especially heinous:

> *Your victim was your wife, she was a woman, and a woman, too, which you had promised to love and respect—but instead of loving and protecting her, you have imbrued your hands in her blood.*

If you had committed it under other circumstances, it might have mitigated your offense . . . You did not cleave her with a club, or stab her with a knife, or shoot her down with a gun upon a sudden impulse of passion, but you drowned her and the evidence shows that you did it in not an instant, that it could not have been done except by your effort and continuous act and with difficulty. In that period you had time to reflect. In that time you must have felt her struggle, you must have felt the throbs, you must have felt the tremor which immediately preceded dissolution.

Whiton instructed McCaffary, who did not confess, to spend his final days repenting. "It is my duty to announce to you that you have but a short time to live," he told the condemned man, "your days are numbered. I feel it is my duty not as a judge, but as your friend, and let me entreat you to spend the remnant of your life in repentance of your sins."

The judge concluded with a thought of the victim.

"The law allows you time to prepare for death, but it is one of the peculiar features of the murderer that he gives his victim no time to prepare for death. I was not acquainted with your victim. I know not whether she was prepared or not. I only know that no time was given her by you."

The day of the execution, August 21, 1851, was a circus.

"Early in the morning carriages flocked into the city," wrote C. Latham Sholes, editor of the *Kenosha Telegraph*. A "morbidly excited" crowd of more than three thousand people gathered around the scaffold on a sandy knoll at the edge of town.

McCaffary was led from jail by a parade of numerous officials, as well as the Kenosha City Guard, decked out in full dress uniform with fixed bayonets.

The crowd had to be quieted so McCaffary could offer his penance. He knelt in prayer with a priest for ten minutes.

According to custom, the prisoner was given the opportunity for final words. McCaffary confessed for the first time, and deputies repeated the killer's statement to the crowd: "I was the cause of the death of my wife, and hope my fate will be a warning to you all. I forgive all my enemies. I forgive all the witnesses against me."

The prisoner was blindfolded and a hood was placed over his head. Then he waited. And waited. Finally, at 1:00 P.M., the execution time set by the governor, the sheriff walked across the gallows and tripped a spring.

Death came by slow strangulation. The primitive method used by authorities hoisted McCaffary into the air rather than dropping him through a trapdoor. He struggled for five minutes. After a few more minutes, physicians noted that his pulse was only slightly reduced. McCaffary lived at least another ten minutes while dangling above the gallows.

Sholes railed against the execution in his newspaper:

> *The last agony is over. The crowd has been indulged in its insane passion for the sight of a judicially murdered man. McCaffary murdered his wife without the sanction of the Law, and McCaffary has been murdered according to law. We do not complain that the law has been enforced. We complain that the law exists. . . . We hope this will be the last execution that shall ever disgrace the mercy-expecting citizens of the State of Wisconsin.*

It was, and Wisconsin has prohibited the death penalty for 151 years, longer than any other state in the nation.

As a legislator, Sholes advocated strongly for the Death Penalty Repeal Act, signed into law by Governor Farwell on July 10, 1853. (Though, in the years immediately following the repeal, vigilante mobs were in the habit of lynching murder suspects.)

In the end, McCaffary repented just as the judge had asked, and he reportedly became deeply religious. His eleventh-hour conversion was due partly to the long dark nights in jail when McCaffary believed the spirit of his dead wife was haunting him.

John McCaffary was buried in Green Ridge Cemetery, Kenosha.

The McCaffarys' house on Court Street is a registered historic landmark.

STRIKING A BLOW FOR FREEDOM

- 1854 -

ON A COOL MARCH NIGHT NEAR the Root River in Racine, Joshua Glover was playing cards inside his shanty when three men burst through the door. One of the men identified Glover by name. When Glover tried to flee, he was pistol-whipped and, with a boot on his neck, handcuffed, then thrown into the back of a wagon.

Two of the men were federal marshals.

The arrest of Glover, an escaped slave from Missouri, set into motion a chain of events that sparked outrage across the nation, rallying antislavery activists toward the first serious challenge of the Fugitive Slave Act of 1850.

After escaping from slavery, Glover had found work with an abolitionist at a Racine sawmill. But then his former master (the man who had identified Glover to marshals the night of his arrest), ordered his return in accordance with the Fugitive Slave Act, a federal decree that allowed slave owners to retrieve escaped slaves from free states.

The marshals had made their way to Racine under the cover of darkness, knowing that local opposition to slavery ran deep. Once Glover was apprehended, March 10, 1854, the men took him to Milwaukee's courthouse jail, where they believed their prisoner would be secure.

By word of mouth, by telegraph, by the tolling of church bells, news of Glover's arrest roused the countryside. The next morning a crowd had gathered at the Racine courthouse. From there, a hundred ardent abolitionists boarded a boat to Milwaukee, parading to the jail and causing a stir. A Milwaukee abolitionist named Sherman Booth received word of the arrest and took to his horse, riding through the streets to rally the townspeople.

By 2:00 P.M. hundreds of determined citizens were gathered at the jail. Booth and a series of speakers stirred the crowd to an angry froth with their fiery rhetoric. From the authorities, they demanded a writ of habeas corpus—Glover's right to due process and a trial by jury. A local judge had issued a writ in support, but a federal judge had overruled him, arguing that violations of the fugitive slave law fell under the jurisdiction of the United States courts.

Tensions escalated throughout the afternoon. By 6:00 P.M. the crowd was demanding the keys to the jail. The sheriff refused.

Across the square, piles of lumber awaited the construction of St. John's Cathedral. A large beam was procured from the site and used as a battering ram to force the jailhouse door open. Amid the protection of the cheering crowd, the liberated Glover was spirited into a wagon and rushed out of town. He disappeared on the Underground Railroad somewhere near Waukesha and within days he was in Canada, a free man once again.

Repercussions were felt across the country. Abolitionists were emboldened.

In Wisconsin a complicated series of far-reaching legal battles began with the arrest of Sherman Booth, the most visible and militant abolitionist involved in freeing Glover. He was taken into custody by federal authorities, but was released when the Wisconsin Supreme Court struck down the Fugitive Slave Act, causing a national furor. The argument made by Booth's lawyer against the act—"The priceless benefits of freedom should be surrounded by every safeguard, and protected from encroachment or invasion, every man worthy to enjoy its blessings . . ."—became widely published throughout the North.

In 1855 Booth was arrested again and tried in federal district court in Madison, where he was sentenced to prison. (The federal district judge was called an "old granny and a miserable doughface" by one newspaper.) Again, the Wisconsin Supreme Court stepped in to assert its jurisdiction and ordered Booth's release.

The legal wrangling continued for four years. When the United States Supreme Court ordered a copy of the state proceedings for review, the Wisconsin court simply ignored the request. The feds assumed jurisdiction in 1857, despite the state's tactics, and two years later reversed the decision of the Wisconsin court.

In 1859 Booth was arrested yet again, only to be "liberated" from a Milwaukee jail by friends. He caught a train to Waupun and continued his crusade against slavery.

A marshal caught up to him three days later in Ripon as Booth was giving a speech. It was the wrong place at the wrong time for the marshal. As the marshal tried to make his arrest, the crowd rushed the stage, with cries of "shoot him!" During the ensuing melee, Booth was whisked into hiding.

Booth evaded capture for the next two months, protected by cadres of armed supporters known as Wide–Awakes.

As the nation became a cauldron boiling over with political tempers, Booth's exploits—some real, some exaggerated—were trumpeted by newspapers. He was characterized as a saint or a child molester depending on the persuasion of the newspaper.

For a while Booth stayed at a home in southern Winnebago County. The authorities made another attempt to apprehend him, but a posse of angry farmers defended the property with pitchforks and shotguns.

"What is the character of [these] men?" wrote the *Ripon Times* in support of Booth and his army. "They are our farmers, our mechanics, our students—men, young and old, of sobriety, integrity, and honor—men who in all the ordinary routine of life are the best neighbors and citizens. Moreover they are persons of strong moral convictions, and uncompromising in their devotion to their principles."

Booth's heroic cat-and-mouse game ended on October 8, 1860, when he was apprehended in Berlin. He would remain in jail until pardoned the following March. By then the nation was on the brink of civil war and Abraham Lincoln, an abolitionist, had assumed the presidency. Once pardoned, Booth used his fame to encourage Union army enlistments throughout the Midwest.

After the war, the decades rolled by and Booth continued to speak out on the issues of the day, but nothing came close to the epic struggles of the 1850s.

On the night of March 11, 1897—the anniversary of Joshua Glover's rescue—the eighty-five-year-old Sherman Booth was invited to speak in the Assembly Chamber of the Wisconsin capitol. It was to be his last public appearance.

"Hesitatingly he sketched the first phrases," according to one written account. "But as he warmed to his subject, there came a glint in his eyes, a vigor in his voice and an animation of spirit which transported him to the days of the 'Underground Railroad' when he was its outstanding station master."

For one last time, Sherman Booth was the thundering crusader in a great moral conflict.

"There was something higher than decisions of courts on the constitutionality of or unconstitutionality of the Fugitive Slave Act," he said, shaking his fist. "It was the old battle—not yet ended—between freedom and slavery; between the rights of the toiling many and the special privileges of the aristocratic few. It was the outlawed right against despotic might; it was human justice against arbitrary power; it was divine mercy against infernal cruelty; it was the refining spirit of humanity!"

Booth died August 11, 1904, and was buried in Milwaukee's Forest Home Cemetery. In 2006 the National Park Service named Milwaukee's Cathedral Square as an official Underground Railroad site. The square is where residents first grabbed a beam from the cathedral's construction and struck a blow felt across the land.

COMMIES, SWINGERS, AND
REPUBLICANS, OH MY!

- 1854 -

BADGER STATE RESIDENTS WHO PAID ATTENTION DURING their fourth grade Wisconsin history class have already learned that Ripon was once the midwestern home of that great political movement, communism.

Whoa, friends of John Birch, settle down. Here's the story . . .

In Wisconsin, the small town of Ripon is famous as the birthplace of the Republican Party. (Just don't ask folks in Michigan for their opinion.) But less widely known is the quirky commune established before the Grand Old Party was either grand or old. Add to the mix a few swingers and spiritualists, and it must have been dang interesting at the Saturday night cotillion.

After a meeting in Kenosha, the young and impressionable Warren Chase became a Fourierite, a follower of French socialist Charles Fourier. Fourier's theories were one of many "isms" in vogue following America's economic collapse in the 1830s. Chase organized a stock sale and with the eight hundred dollars in proceeds, he bought the land where Ripon is located today. Nearly two hundred people eventually moved there. Fourier's complicated plan of replacing economic classes for a system of credits according to usefulness was instituted by Chase.

A "long house" was constructed and the commune thrived. Everything seemed hunky-dory. That is, until all sorts of individualists began surfacing, from free-love devotees to spiritualists. Some of the commies just didn't like the others and wanted to eat alone.

As nearby farmland became settled, the dream of individual ownership and the prospect of making money the old-fashioned way—through speculation—finished Chase's experiment after six years. In a decidedly capitalistic finale, more than forty thousand dollars in dividends from the property sale was paid out to commune members.

Chase moved around the country and eventually settled in California, where, as a devout spiritualist, he communed only with the dead.

Republicans have fared a bit better.

As Chase's commune was folding, the matter of slavery was pushing everything else off the front page, including novel little experiments like Fourierism. The proverbial line in the sand was drawn when the Kansas–Nebraska bill was introduced in early 1854, proposing the expansion of slavery based on popular vote in those territories. The measure outraged antislavery forces.

At the time, the political landscape was a hodgepodge of groups, including the Free Soil Party, Whigs, Conscience Whigs, Democrats, and Anti-Nebraska Democrats.

Into this confusing mix, entered Alvan Earle Bovay, a Ripon lawyer, Democrat, and opponent of the Kansas–Nebraska bill.

Bovay called a meeting on March 20, 1854. From the Republican National Committee's (RNC) official history: "Meeting in a Congregational church in Ripon, Wis., [Bovay] helped establish a party that represented the interests of the North and the abolitionists by merging two fundamental issues: free land and preventing the spread of slavery into the Western territories."

One of the people attending the meeting was George F. Lynch, who later reminisced about the gathering in a newspaper article. "I remember just as well as if it were yesterday," wrote Lynch, then eighty years old.

> *Alvan E. Bovay and sixteen others of us met in the little old school house. My sister was teacher of the school, and after she had dismissed her pupils that afternoon, Bovay arranged for the political meeting. He was the brainiest man in the entire community, and the thought of giving to the proposed new political party, which would combine the elements of all parties that were opposed to the extension of slavery, the name 'Republican' had long been in his mind.*
>
> *He had suggested it to Horace Greeley, with whom he was on intimate terms, and who was then editor of* The New York Tribune, *the leading Whig organ in the country. But it was left for that little school house meeting of ours to give the party its birth. . . .*
>
> *At the meeting I suggested that we call our party 'Democrat–Republican,' and there were other suggestions, but Bovay won out. And it was largely due to his facile pen and his connection with the leading*

newspapers in the country that the quarrel inside of the Democratic party resulted in having the name 'Republican' formally adopted by the new party first in Wisconsin, then in Maine, and in Michigan, and later throughout the country.

So there it is. Ripon, Wisconsin—birthplace of the Republican Party.

Well, probably.

Problem is, meetings like this were happening all over the place as outrage against the Kansas–Nebraska bill exploded. Bovay was one of countless leaders marshalling antislavery sentiment in the North, and many meetings advocated the organization of a new party to protest the bill.

But it is Bovay's relationship with Greeley, the man accepted as first promoting the Republican moniker in his paper, that allowed Ripon to earn its bragging rights as birthplace of the Republican Party.

A few months after the Ripon meeting, the town of Jackson, Michigan, hosted a Republican Party convention. The first national convention of the party was held in Pittsburgh in 1856. (The party's nominee, John C. Fremont, ran under the banner, "Free soil, free labor, free speech, free men, Fremont." Cool slogan. Didn't get him elected.)

"Whether one accepts Wisconsin's claim depends largely on what one means by the words 'birthplace' and 'party,'" according to the Wisconsin Historical Society. "Modern reference books, while acknowledging the ambiguity, usually cite Ripon as the birthplace of the organized movement to form the party. If not born in Ripon, the party was at least conceived there."

And so while Jackson, Michigan, has always made a stink about being the birthplace of the Republican Party, we called it first.

OUR PRIZE-WINNING DAIRY AIR

- 1872 -

IN THE EARLY YEARS OF STATEHOOD, Wisconsin farmers were churning butter the only way they knew how, the way it had always been churned . . . in a filthy barn, with milk from cows that had been fed garbage. Literally.

"The churning process was casual and unsanitary, and families made no effort to control what the cow ate," according to the *Wisconsin Magazine of History.* "As a result, many unwholesome odors—from dirty laundry to wild onions and garlic—found their way into the butter."

To make things worse, according to the state dairy and food commissioner, the typical farmer "has dung beneath him, behind him, in front of him and above him and manipulates a filthy surface above the milk pail."

The resulting milk and butter was mixed indiscriminately into barrels and shipped unrefrigerated. The entire process—from sewage-ridden, fly-infested barns to cross-contaminated barrels—occurred without sanitation or inspection. By the time Wisconsin butter reached consumers, it was often inedible. In fact, it was sold in Chicago by the hundred-weight as wagon-wheel grease.

America's Dairyland, eh? Not a bad title considering Wisconsin butter was once so nasty it was used to grease axles.

To get from there to here took a disaster, an agricultural revolution, and the vision of a man who drove a dairy herd right into the governor's office—figuratively speaking, of course.

It started with pestilence, one of the four horsemen of the Apocalypse (fortunately, the other three horsemen were somewhere else—Illinois maybe). Chinch bugs ravaged our wheat crops in the late 1860s. Wisconsin was the third-largest wheat producer in the nation at the time. The crops failed, the soil was shot, new and better lands opened west of Wisconsin, and that was that.

Enter William Dempster Hoard, a Yankee who had found his calling in agricultural journalism. After serving in the Civil War, Hoard started the *Jefferson County Union* in south central Wisconsin.

According to Norman Risjord, a history professor at the University of Wisconsin, "Hoard knew that quality controls for the dairy products most easily transported, butter and cheese, were paramount."

And Hoard knew that when it came to dairy farming, everything started with the cow.

He founded an association of dairymen in 1872 to spread the word to friends and neighbors about the benefits of high-quality milk, starting with TLC for Bessie.

"To him who loveth the cow," Hoard wrote, "to him shall all other things be added—feed, ensilage, butter, more grasses, more prosperity, happier homes, and greater wealth."

This was an entirely foreign concept to most farmers. A dairy cow or two was typically used to support a family, not as part of an industry. Some farmers, in fact, were downright hostile to the idea of turning a profit. Besides, trying to ship and sell surplus milk before it spoiled was nearly impossible.

The answer, the linchpin to the entire dairy revolution, Hoard knew, was cheese. It required less refrigeration. Lifting the model from his native New York, Hoard promoted the idea of local cheese factories whereby farmers could sell their milk locally. Then he embraced the use of ice-refrigerated cars to ship the product east.

Butter and cheese cooperatives. A board of trade. The Wisconsin Dairymen's Association. *Hoard's Dairyman* trade journal. Marketing in New York, Boston, even Great Britain. All the pieces were in place for a revolution, and within a decade Wisconsin dairy products had earned an international reputation for their quality.

And farmers jumped at the opportunity, right?

Nah.

"Notoriously poor rural roads made transporting milk from farm to [cheese] factory hazardous and tedious," according to the *History of Wisconsin, Volume IV.* "Highly individualistic farmers, used to working at their own pace and constrained only by the weather, had a difficult time adjusting to the schedule and rhythm of 'the system.' Factory managers demanded standards of quality and caused many dairymen to grumble."

Farmers would bust a wagon wheel hauling milk to the factory only to find, after they finally arrived, that their partially spoiled product didn't meet the new quality standards, and they were not happy.

Hoard enlisted the help of the University of Wisconsin. It was another brilliant stroke, the type of partnership we take for granted today but one that was a strange concept in the 1880s. Academia was reluctant, fearing a proliferation of—gasp!—*vocational* courses.

The courses were created nevertheless, and science and technology were applied to farming methods. Eventually the College of Agriculture opened its doors in 1891—with a big boost from *Governor* Hoard. That's right, Hoard had become so well known for saving Wisconsin agriculture that the "cow editor" was elected to office in 1888.

Between 1890 and 1912 Wisconsin butter production nearly doubled, and its value tripled; cheese production rose 500 percent, and its value increased more than 800 percent.

"So complete was this metamorphosis by 1914 that Wisconsin outstripped any other single state in milk production and the making of butter and cheese," according to the *History of Wisconsin.* "So successful were the collaborative efforts of dairy farmers, the University of Wisconsin's College of Agriculture, and state government that they established a powerful precedent for similar co-operative endeavors involving private interest groups, the university, and the state."

This is known as the Wisconsin Idea, a model replicated just about everywhere. The Badger State had become America's Dairyland, while pioneering a concept that would change the world.

That's good work, Mr. Hoard.

Today Wisconsin no longer rules the dairy world as far as quantity goes. Other states produce more milk and cheese. Other places might even take a top honor or two at the prestigious World Championship Cheese Contest. But the event itself is still held in Madison. There's no other rightful home for it. More to the point, our cheeses dominate the competition's fifty categories in a resounding affirmation of quality over quantity. In a recent championship, Wisconsin cheese producers took seventeen gold medals, twenty-one silver medals, and eighteen bronze medals. The next best state took two gold medals.

Our license plate says AMERICA'S DAIRYLAND, so it must be true.

One last case in point. When you watch a sporting event in Wisconsin, the television camera inevitably pans the crowd for people wearing those foam cheese-wedge hats. Regardless of how you feel about the silly hats, "cheesehead" is a term universally known, and it's used alternately as a badge of honor and a humorous put down.

Anyway, sure beats edible axle grease. Try wearing *that* on your head.

HOLOCAUST

- 1871 -

AT ABOUT 8:30 P.M. ON OCTOBER 8, 1871, Peshtigo's Catholic priest, Father Peter Pernin, looked toward the west and saw a "dense cloud of smoke overhanging the earth, a vivid red reflection of immense extent, and then suddenly struck on my ear . . . a distant roaring, yet muffled sound, announcing that the elements were in commotion somewhere. . . . The wind, forerunner of the tempest, was increasing in violence, the redness in the sky deepening, and the roaring sound like thunder seemed almost upon us."

Pernin set his horse free.

Black balls of fire the size of balloons were carried by gale-force winds. The balls exploded upon contact. One eyewitness told of seeing a family huddled in the center of a farm field when one of the balls made a direct hit, killing the entire clan.

Then the firestorm struck.

"The air was no longer fit to breathe, full as it was of sand, dust, ashes, cinders, sparks, smoke and fire," Pernin wrote. "It was almost impossible to keep one's eyes unclosed, to distinguish the road, or to recognize people, though the way was crowded with pedestrians, as well as vehicles crossing and crashing against each other in the general flight."

Villagers instinctively fled to the Peshtigo River. Father Pernin continued to describe the scene:

> *The neighing of horses, falling of chimneys, crashing of uprooted trees, roaring and whistling of the wind, crackling of fire as it ran with lightening-like rapidity from house to house—all sounds were there save that of the human voice. People seemed stricken dumb by terror. They jostled each other without exchanging look, word, or counsel. The silence of the tomb reigned among the living; nature alone lifted up its voice and spoke.*

The temperature in the fire's midst reached between 1,500 and 2,000 degrees Fahrenheit. It created its own atmospheric circulation, generating high winds—a hurricane of fire. The flames consumed available oxygen. Buildings exploded. People burst into flames.

Those who made it to the river struggled between suffocation above the water and drowning below.

"The air itself was on fire," wrote Pernin. "Our heads were in continual danger." Refugees used wet blankets to cover their heads, but those too burst into flames when exposed to the air.

Pernin tells of a woman who reached the river with a bundle of linen pressed to her chest. "O horror!" he wrote. "On opening these wraps to look at the face of her child, it was not there. It must have slipped from her grasp in the hurried flight." Pernin attempted to console the woman who, he later learned, drowned herself.

Others stood on the riverbank "motionless as statues, some with eyes staring, upturned toward heaven, and tongues protruded," resigned to their fate in the belief that it was the end of the world.

For five hours the people in the river tried to cling to life, some dying by drowning and exposure. One man had protected his two young siblings in the river only to discover, carrying them to shore, that they had died from hypothermia.

The fire eventually reached the waters of Green Bay and burned itself out. The winds died down. Rain began to fall and temperatures plunged. After surviving a death by fire, people began dying from the cold.

Father Pernin, suffering a violent chill after leaving the water, burrowed into the hot sand to warm himself.

The year 1871 was marked by a severe drought in the upper Midwest. Combined with the common lumber practice of clear-cutting—taking every available tree and leaving the landscape covered with nothing but stumps and slash piles—the conditions in northeast Wisconsin were a tinder box waiting for a spark. The inevitable, possibly caused by spontaneous combustion, happened on the night of October 8.

Sixteen towns were damaged or destroyed, including locations in Door County on the other side of Green Bay.

How many people died in the Peshtigo fire will never be known. The population included many native peoples, itinerant workers (lumberjacks and mill workers), and immigrant homesteaders who had not been counted in the census taken a year earlier.

In the Peshtigo cemetery, small graveside placards placed by the local historical society tell the stories. At the McGregor monument: "In the course of the fire the boarding house and all its occupants were reduced to ashes, making recognition impossible. Dan McGregor's watch was found and the hands indicated five minutes after ten.

It is believed that this monument is a memorial to those names it bears and that no bodies were buried here."

At the Kelly family gravesite: "Terrance Kelly, his wife and four children became separated, voices could not be heard over the roar of the fire. The next day Mr. Kelly and child were found dead nearly a mile from the farm, the mother and another child were safe, the other children were found sleeping in each others arms near the farm."

Orphaned children were adopted informally by other families and took new surnames. Many survivors lived the rest of their lives with disfiguring scars. The pain and heartbreak experienced by the survivors no doubt traveled down through the years, creating feelings of sadness and depression long after the fire had faded.

Like everything else, Peshtigo's Congregational Church was lost. The church cemetery, located next to the former building, was opened to the community. Wagons carrying the dead lined up for three miles. Survivors and relief workers accompanied the remains of loved ones, neighbors, strangers, and at least 350 bodies that could not be identified.

As many as 2,400 people were incinerated in the fire. In terms of lives lost, it remains the worst wildfire in our nation's history.

At the time some people believed it was the end of the world. For many it was. It's not uncommon when folks are researching families in northeast Wisconsin to find a strange void in the lineage in the late-nineteenth century. In many cases, entire families, especially in the Oconto County area, just vanished. The family trees follow a typical pattern until 1871, then . . . nothing.

The "Peshtigo Fire," as it came to be known—referring to the Oconto County community that suffered the worst—will always be overshadowed by the Chicago Fire, a tragic yet smaller conflagration that ironically occurred on exactly the same day. Chicago, after all, was a major city with communication to the rest of the world, while Oconto County was a wilderness with one telegraph line—a line destroyed by the fire. By the time news of Peshtigo's disaster reached Wisconsin Governor Lucius Fairchild, he was in Chicago helping relief efforts there.

Still, Peshtigo stands out. The reach of the fire—2,400 square miles, or 1.5 million acres—is still astounding, and the toll it took in human life (eight hundred people dying in Peshtigo alone, nearly half of the town's population) is heartbreaking.

No big-city headlines, no legends about a cow kicking over a lantern, no folk songs. Just Hell on Earth.

Today the Peshtigo cemetery looks like virtually any other pioneer graveyard found in small towns across the land. Shade trees provide cover from the summer heat. Old headstones lean into the elements. Squirrels and birds frolic along the picket fences.

It's not until visitors reach a signpost in the middle of the cemetery that the serenity is broken and the enormity of what happened begins to take hold. What the sign says is brutally simple: MASS GRAVES.

The marker for those graves and the weather-beaten headstones are all that stand today to tell the story.

SATURDAY AFTERNOON DAREDEVIL

- 1882 -

"It was a cold November morning," one of the boys recalled later. "A light snow had fallen during the night, and the morning air was crisp and clear."

The entourage of seven, led by three young brothers, loaded trunks full of costumes and musical instruments and began the fifteen-mile wagon ride to Sauk City. From there they would catch the train to Mazomanie, only one stop down the Wisconsin River but far enough away from Baraboo, their home, so that nobody would recognize them.

Their "advance man" had papered Mazomanie with flyers. "Do not fail to see the many attractions presented by this company. See our Priseworthy [sic] and Unequalled Program."

For the Ringling brothers—especially for Al, the oldest brother—it was the culmination of a lifelong dream. Their "hall show" in Mazomanie was not the full circus Al had envisioned, but he knew that would come eventually. He had spent his entire life preparing for the day when the Ringling name would appear at the top of the bill. As a child, Al had led "parades" through town to promote his backyard "circus"—a menagerie of common animals "from Timbuctoo," a little bit of music, and a tightrope demonstration. As a young man working at a Broadhead, Wisconsin, blacksmith shop, Al had wowed spectators with Saturday afternoon daredevil performances, running a line between the tops of two buildings and walking high above the street while balancing a plow on his chin. He later spent four years on the road with various circuses, embracing the grueling lifestyle and perfecting his skills as a juggler, equestrian, and high-wire performer.

Now at age thirty, Al had reached the point where it was make or break. Back home that summer in Baraboo, he decided the most practical way to start was a variety road show. His troupe included two brothers—nineteen-year-old Alf and eighteen-year-old Charles—and four local musicians.

On the evening of November 27, 1882, the group took the stage in Mazomanie. They bombed.

"From the very beginning," Al recalled, "the troupe in its entirety seemed to fly to pieces. It seemed that as if every note from the cornet was a blue one, every tone from the violin a squeak, every blast of the clarinet a shriek, and as if all the different instruments were in a jangle."

Spring Green, Richland Center, Boscobel, Prairie du Chien— the undaunted Ringlings soldiered on. Brother John joined them as they made their way into Minnesota, Iowa, and the Dakota Territory. Al resurrected a promotional trick from his childhood, marching the entourage, instruments blaring, through town before the evening show.

They closed the season after 107 shows, no small accomplishment for a new troupe. "They were snowed in and snowed out; they arrived by train and from the trains by buggy, by horse and sleigh, and on foot," according to the book, *Ringlingville, USA*. Along the way they learned the finer points of scheduling, booking, contracting, advertising, and publicity.

Every year after 1882, Al and his brothers returned home with a bigger show. They made Baraboo their winter headquarters for decades. "Ringlingville," as it became known, grew into a sprawling village overseen by Al. Today it's a major attraction operated by the Wisconsin Historical Society, complete with dazzling acts under a big top.

When Al and his siblings celebrated their twenty-fifth anniversary, their circus, the Ringling Brothers' World's Greatest Shows, accommodated fifteen thousand spectators under big tops, and the circus city covered twelve acres. They opened their 1908 season with a one-month stint at Madison Square Garden. They would go on to clear nearly a million dollars that year, the equivalent of twenty million today.

The Ringling Brothers enterprise became an international giant by running family-friendly shows free of the con men and questionable characters usually associated with circuses. They pioneered the circus parade, allowing millions of people to witness the glitter and glamour for free. They transitioned from performers into some of the savviest and most highly respected business managers of their day.

"The Ringling Brothers succeeded in their quest, far beyond their wildest dreams," said Fred Dahlinger Jr., a former director of the Circus World Museum. "The secret of their achievements was teamwork, facilitated by their personal bonds. It was their mutual respect and trust, not a piece of paper, that empowered them to rise above all competitors."

At their peak, the Ringling Brothers' World's Greatest Shows contained 1,300 employees, 1,000 exotic animals, and 650 horses. They traveled with eighty-four railroad cars and were studied by the

U.S. Army for their efficiency in moving what amounted to a city in a matter of hours.

In 1910 they bought their largest competitor, the Barnum and Bailey circus.

Three months before his death in January 1916, Al Ringling attended the opening of a theater named in his honor. Located on Baraboo's town square, the stunning venue was patterned directly after the opera house at Versailles. The Ringling Brothers financed the construction. The "Al" sparkles yet today, the entertainers on its stage bringing untold enjoyment to the people—just as its namesake dreamt on that chilly November morning so long ago when he packed up a wagon and headed off to Mazomanie.

FIGHTING BOB

- 1904 -

The Stalwarts gathered inside the Fuller Opera House, an ornate gray building with stained glass windows across from the state capitol. They began their march down State Street before noon.

Spectators lined the route. Women in bulky dresses and parasols clutched children clad in knickers and caps. Men anxiously puffed nickel cigars. Rumor had it that ol' Bob was going to confront Spooner's Stalwarts with ruffians who had been residing in the city jail the night before. Violence was possible.

The Stalwarts marched four abreast behind two American flags. They made it down to the convention hall on Lake Mendota without incident, a gaggle of spectators following close behind.

How appropriate that this political convention should be held in the University of Wisconsin's red gymnasium, which resembled a medieval fortress and had been reinforced "not unlike a penal institution" for the convention, according to one participant.

It was May 18, 1904, and it would be the last time Wisconsin candidates for office were chosen by party insiders. After this, voters would determine who made it on the ballot through an open primary system. But for now, control of state politics was still at stake, as well as the national aspirations of a fledgling political reform movement led by Wisconsin's Progressive Republican governor Robert M. La Follette. The conservative Stalwart Republicans, led by the powerful United States senator John C. Spooner, also of Wisconsin, were set to oppose them.

In the months leading up to the convention "each group was determined to annihilate the other and neither was scrupulous about the methods used," according to one historian. A decade of bitter Republican infighting would be settled at the Red Gym that day, changing the course of state and national politics.

Both La Follette and Spooner were graduates of the University of Wisconsin, and both had earlier been elected to federal seats—Spooner to the Senate, La Follette to the House. During their first stint in Washington, Spooner began his ascension among the power brokers while La Follette toiled as a conventional Republican.

Then, out of office for a decade and working as a politically active attorney, La Follette had a life-altering experience that would spur what he characterized as "the crucial period of my public life." Philetus Sawyer, a political brother to Spooner, allegedly offered La Follette a bribe to influence a Dane County judge. Sawyer claimed he was offering La Follette a retainer to represent him. Either way, La Follette was incensed by Sawyer's actions and he became a man determined to smash the reigning political machine.

In the *History of Wisconsin, Volume IV,* John Buenker wrote, "Outwardly calm, outwardly loyal, La Follette played the role of the steadfast party wheelhorse, storing up his resentments for the future." His resentments were found to be justified when he later spoke on behalf of the party ticket led by Spooner in 1892—only to be ousted as Dane County Republican chairman and replaced by Spooner's brother.

Spooner and three other Republicans virtually controlled Congress for the next decade, beginning in 1897. (He declined offers to serve as attorney general in the McKinley administration and secretary of state in the Taft cabinet.)

La Follette continued to work the back door. He approached anyone slighted by Spooner in an appointment or promotion. He quietly assembled a grassroots organization the likes of which had not been seen before in Wisconsin.

La Follette's first arch nemesis, Philetus Sawyer, had died, and Spooner was too busy with his national responsibilities to stymie La Follette's successful run for the governorship in 1900. La Follette was elected as a Progressive Republican and began to wrest control of Wisconsin from the Stalwarts in his party, earning the nickname "Fighting Bob" along the way.

The 1904 nominating convention "became a landmark in Wisconsin's political history," Buenker wrote. "For political sound and fury," the event "set a standard that may never be equaled." Although La Follette and Spooner did not face each other on the convention ballot, the Progressives and the Stalwarts turned the meeting into a fight for control of the party, therefore determining control of the state. (Democrats had little influence at the time.) Also hanging in the balance was the future of the Progressive movement.

When the Stalwarts arrived at the Red Gym, they realized the Progressives had hijacked the venue. Buenker wrote, "The delegates were forced to enter the gymnasium single file through a side entrance at the end of a barbed wire runway patrolled by members of a small army of burly university football players, wrestlers, and fraternity brothers, supplemented by some tough-looking characters recently resident in the Madison city jail."

La Follette called his security force "fine, clean, upright fellows who were physically able to meet any emergency." Most prominent among them were Evan "Strangler" Lewis, a champion wrestler, and "Norsky" Larson, a Badger football star.

Plenty of counterfeit credentials were flying around the gym, but it was the Stalwart delegates who were rejected by the credentials committee and tossed by the Progressive's security men.

"Amidst this atmosphere bristling with all manner of hostile emotions," La Follette saw his slate of Progressive candidates win nomination to the Republican ticket, virtually assuring their victory in the general election. Stalwarts stormed out of the gym and regrouped at the opera house, where they nominated their own ticket, led by Spooner. The opera house meeting "was a great success," according to Stalwarts, and it "stood out in a most favorable contrast with the game warden's carnival" at the Red Gym.

The convention controversy was widely reported, and national attention was directed toward the Wisconsin Progressives. La Follette used the publicity to his full advantage. After the Wisconsin Supreme Court handed down a decision legitimizing the Red Gym convention, progressives took control of the state legislature and "Fighting Bob" La Follette emerged as a national figure of reform.

Things went from bad to worse for the Stalwarts. Even as Spooner was becoming disenchanted with Teddy Roosevelt's reformist policies, La Follette, whose star continued to rise after successfully implementing a progressive platform as governor, was elected to be Spooner's colleague in the Senate in 1906.

Senate tradition dictates that a new member be presented by the senior senator from the state.

"The murmur of the galleries smote the ear" as the men walked through the senate chamber, La Follette wrote his wife Belle. "The vice president requested [Spooner] to present me. He offered me his right wing . . . the oath was administered . . . an audible sigh swept down from the galleries as the tension relaxed . . . I extended to him my hand, and thanked him for his courtesy. The thing was done."

Spooner seated La Follette in the back row, behind the minority party.

Eager to make waves, La Follette ignored the usual yearlong look-and-learn period and asked for an assignment on the most powerful committees. Instead, Spooner gave him chairmanship of the Select Committee to Investigate the Condition of the Potomac Riverfront. "No bill had ever been referred to it and its office was in a remote, dimly lit basement corridor of the Capitol basement," according to one biographer.

But Spooner threw in the towel not long after La Follette arrived. He left the Senate and practiced law until his death in 1919. The old Stalwart was buried in Madison's Forest Hill Cemetery without fanfare.

La Follette, despite his seat on the back row, emerged as the leader of an unofficial caucus of populist "insurgents" who challenged the Republican Party on a range of issues. He formed the National Progressive Republican League in 1911 and increasingly sided with "radicals" and underdogs of all stripes, culminating in his third-party presidential campaign of 1924, which garnered 17 percent of the vote.

Spooner's name faded, while La Follette became one of the most famous figures in Wisconsin political history (thanks in no small part to his sons Bob Jr., and Phil, both successful politicians in their own rights).

Robert M. La Follette died less than a year after his Presidential campaign.

"No funeral cortege into the West, since the return of the martyred Lincoln to Springfield, has witnessed such an outpouring of grief," wrote one reporter as the senator returned from Washington for the last time. La Follette was carried aboard the Commonwealth, the train used for his presidential campaign.

Tens of thousands filed past his casket in the state capitol rotunda. The streets were jammed six-deep as the hearse slowly made its way to the cemetery.

As the procession entered Forest Hill Cemetery, one of the first monuments inside the gates bore the name John C. Spooner.

As in life, John Spooner is located to the right of Bob La Follette, but at least the two men are far enough apart to avoid raising the dead.

ASSASSIN!

- 1912 -

JOHN SCHRANK COULD NOT GET THIS DREAM out of his mind. The twenty-fifth president of the United States, William McKinley, lying dead, cut down by an assassin's bullet. Schrank could see it all so clearly. The black draperies, the ornate coffin, the pallid remains of the president. Then McKinley would sit up in his coffin.

"This is my murderer," the slain president said to Schrank, pointing to a man dressed like a monk. "Avenge my death."

The monk was Teddy Roosevelt.

Not the kind of dream easily forgotten, particularly by Schrank, an off-kilter New York City saloonkeeper. In another delusional episode, Schrank felt a tap on his shoulder. "Do not let a murderer sit in the president's chair," the voice intoned. Schrank turned around to find the ghostly form of McKinley behind him.

Soon afterward, John Schrank left New York City armed with a .38-caliber Smith & Wesson pistol.

Meanwhile, Teddy Roosevelt was on the stump again. He had succeeded McKinley in the Oval Office from 1901 to 1908. After a hiatus, which included an African safari, Roosevelt, the ol' Rough Rider, was campaigning for a third term, this time on the Progressive ticket.

Roosevelt remained popular in retirement, but his new ticket—he called it the Bull Moose Party—had a problem, specifically Robert "Fighting Bob" La Follette. The Progressive United States senator from Wisconsin had prepared for a 1912 presidential run believing he had Roosevelt's endorsement. When Roosevelt threw his hat in the ring at the last minute and grabbed the Progressive banner, La Follette was incensed. (The two men had a tenuous relationship anyway. La Follette saw Roosevelt as a reactionary, and Roosevelt considered La Follette a Socialist.) As the campaign hit the homestretch, La Follette wrote a series of scathing articles detailing Roosevelt's "betrayal" of Progressive causes.

When Roosevelt's campaign headed to Wisconsin to salvage his Progressive base of voters, John Schrank, moved by the voices in his head, followed.

Roosevelt reached Milwaukee's Hotel Gilpatrick, at the corner of Kilbourn & Third Street, on October 14. The candidate ate dinner with advisors in a private dining room.

Schrank waited calmly in the lobby. About 8:00 P.M. Roosevelt began making his way through the hotel. Schrank pushed his way through the crowd outside and waited next to the candidate's automobile.

The crowd cheered when the candidate exited the hotel. As he reached the vehicle, Roosevelt stepped up on the floorboard and turned to acknowledge the onlookers. Schrank aimed his pistol at Roosevelt's head. The two men were only a few feet apart. A spectator next to the gunman swung his arm across Schrank's just as the pistol fired.

Roosevelt was thrown backward by the shot. One of his aides quickly pounced on the would-be assassin.

In the chaos that followed, the crowd assumed Schrank had succeeded. They began pummeling him, and cries of "Kill him!" and "Lynch him!" filled the air. Men scattered to find rope.

Roosevelt felt like he had been kicked by a horse, but managed to struggle to his feet to calm the mob. "Don't hurt the poor creature," he yelled.

Roosevelt waved his hat in the air and the crowd erupted in cheers, enabling four policemen to fight their way into the melee and grab Schrank, who was hustled into the hotel and secured in the kitchen while bellboys kept the crowd at bay.

Roosevelt was bloodied and shaken from a gunshot wound to the chest. Having treated battlefield wounds during the Spanish–American War, he induced coughing to see if he was bleeding internally. Famously, after his self-exam proved negative, Roosevelt rebuffed those who begged him to go to a hospital.

"I'm going to make that speech if it's the last thing on earth I do," he told his advisors in the vehicle. With that, the car sped away to the Milwaukee Auditorium three blocks away.

The ten thousand people who had gathered for his speech had no inkling of what had transpired minutes earlier.

A request for doctors was made among the audience. Two men volunteered and were taken backstage, but Roosevelt and his entourage appeared moments later to the cheers of the unwitting crowd.

In a trembling voice, an aide introduced Roosevelt as someone who embodied the Democratic qualities of Jefferson and the Republican qualities of Lincoln. "As he left his hotel a dastardly hand raised a revolver at the colonel," said his aide, "and he will speak to you, though there is a bullet somewhere in his breast."

The audience remained silent.

Roosevelt stood, smiled, and announced, "I don't know whether you fully understand that I have just been shot, but it takes more than that to kill a Bull Moose!"

"There is where the bullet went through—and it probably saved me from it going into my heart," he said, holding his speech manuscript aloft. "The bullet is in me now, so that I cannot make a very long speech, but I will try my best." The former president's remarkable performance that night—his shirt was bloodied and he fought off fainting several times—was reported worldwide in banner headlines.

"I have altogether too important things to think of to feel any concern over my own death; and now I cannot speak to you insincerely within five minutes of being shot. I am telling you the literal truth when I say that my concern is for many other things. It is not in the least for my own life."

But La Follette supporters had packed the auditorium that night, and they caused a disturbance with each mention of the senator's name. Despite Roosevelt's condition, his speech was interrupted five times due to pro-La Follette demonstrations. Finally, the candidate was able to provide a litany of Progressive issues that he and La Follette had championed. He also produced a 1909 article from La Follette's magazine lauding the former president. (He had an aide read the article.)

Roosevelt finished his speech ninety minutes later. Spectators swarmed the candidate. "For a few moments, it looked as though he might suffer because of his throng of admirers," noted a correspondent for the *Milwaukee Sentinel.*

Making no attempt to shield himself from the crowd, the candidate vigorously boarded the *Mayflower,* his private campaign train waiting at the Northwestern Depot at the foot of Wisconsin Avenue.

"Now for a shave," he told his staff.

"But surely, you do not mean that," replied his doctor. "I certainly do."

At 1:00 A.M. on October 15, 1912, Roosevelt departed for a Chicago hospital. He was released weeks later, only days before the

November election. The Bull Moose campaign had ended prematurely in Milwaukee.

Whatever sympathy existed for the wounded former president did not translate into votes. Roosevelt lost to Woodrow Wilson (though he did finish ahead of incumbent President William Howard Taft).

In Wisconsin, the place of his near-assassination, Roosevelt finished a distant third—the rift between he and Progressive favorite La Follette never more apparent.

Roosevelt once told reporters that he would return fire if ever confronted by an assassin, and he frequently carried a gun. Not so that night in Milwaukee.

Schrank was never tried. Judged insane, he died in the Central State Hospital in Waupun, in 1943.

"I did not care a rap for being shot," Roosevelt said later. "It is a trade risk, which every prominent public man ought to accept as a matter of course."

The auditorium where the bloodied candidate gave his speech underwent a forty-two million dollar redesign in 2003. It is now the Milwaukee Theater. The Hotel Gilpatrick at the corner of Kilbourn and Third Street closed in 1941 and was demolished.

MAYHEM AT TALIESIN

- 1914 -

IT WAS NOON ON A SATURDAY in mid-August, and architect Frank Lloyd Wright was in Chicago, finishing his Midway Gardens project. Back in Spring Green, Wisconsin, at a home that Wright had named "Taliesin," his companion Martha "Mamah" Cheney and her two children were sitting down for lunch on the porch. Wright's foreman and tradesmen had gathered to eat in a nearby dining room.

As usual, the male servant, Julian Carlton, served dinner. But then he returned to the dining room moments later and asked permission to use some gasoline on a carpet stain. Soon the staff heard splashing noises against the closed dining room door, and noticed liquid seeping out from underneath. Then fire exploded in the doorway.

Escaping the flames, three members of the staff charged through the glass plating which framed the door. Carlton was waiting with the hatchet. He missed his first victim, Herbert Fritz, then struck a second man, William Weston (who would survive his wounds), and killed the third man, Emil Brodelle, with a direct blow to the head.

The others in the dining room made their way through the fire, not knowing what awaited them on the other side. Again with the hatchet, Carlton attacked Thomas Brunker, Ernest Weston (the thirteen-year-old son of William Weston), and David Lindblom. All three survived the initial attack but perished later from their wounds and burns.

In the brief period before the men attempted to escape from the dining room, Carlton had run to the porch and begun his killing spree on Mamah and her children. Mamah and John Cheney never made it out of their chairs. Young Martha Cheney, struck at least four times, had managed to escape, but she'd been badly burned and died later that night.

Fire began to consume part of the house. Herbert Fritz and the mortally wounded David Lindblom went to a neighboring farm and phoned for help.

When neighbors responded to the alarm, they found seven victims either dead or dying. At 5:30 P.M., Carlton was found hiding in the boiler area. Strangely, his wife was later found dressed in her best clothes, walking on the road to Spring Green.

The events of August 15, 1914, would have made news under any circumstances, but the fact that the gruesome slaying of seven people occurred at the home of a famous architect—and among the victims were Frank Lloyd Wright's partner in a scandalous love affair and her two children—spurred headlines worldwide, momentarily pushing aside news of the great war engulfing Europe.

Martha Borthwick Cheney met Frank Lloyd Wright through the architect's first wife, Catherine, in Chicago in the early 1900s. Martha's husband, electrical engineer Edwin Cheney, soon commissioned Wright to build a home in Oak Park, Illinois.

Following the home's completion in 1905, Wright and Martha Cheney began an affair that shocked conventional society. Wright felt that his family life at that time "conspired against the freedom to which I had come to feel every soul was entitled." The couple left their respective families in Chicago and traveled around the globe for more than a year. Neither was divorced. Wright called it a "voluntary exile into the uncharted and unknown."

Newspapers called it something else, denouncing the couple's affair and even suggesting that Wright should be arrested for immorality.

Martha, known as "Mamah," eventually divorced Edwin Cheney in 1911, but Catherine Wright refused, believing her husband would come to his senses and return to their marriage (he never did, and Catherine finally granted him a divorce in 1922).

Between the bad press and the couple flaunting their "free love" relationship, Wright's career suffered dramatically. Such considerations were of little concern to the lovebirds, however, and Wright soon began building his dream home for Mamah and her two children, young Martha and John Cheney. By the summer of 1914, the couple had been together for more than five tumultuous years, and Taliesin had gone from blueprint to reality. The home was nestled in southern Wisconsin's rolling hills, where Wright's grandparents had settled during the Civil War.

Julian Carlton and his wife had been servants at Taliesin for only a short time that summer. In the days leading up to August 15, Carlton's wife noticed Julian acting strangely. He purchased a bottle of acid in town and began carrying a hatchet to bed. Known for his hot temper, Carlton apparently had run-ins with Mamah and members of the Taliesin staff days before the massacre. Evidently the couple had been given notice to leave.

After the bloody massacre, Carlton was taken into custody and transported to the county jail in Dodgeville. On the streets outside, the sheriff and his deputies stood with weapons drawn to fend off an angry mob that had been gathering throughout the day.

Wright arrived home by train late in the night. Edwin Cheney, the former husband of Mamah, was on the same train, traveling to Spring Green to retrieve his children's bodies and bring them back to Chicago for burial.

The *Dodgeville Chronicle* reported that the servant "with a shingling hatchet added the final crimson chapter to the free love romance of Frank Lloyd Wright, the architect, and his soulmate, Mrs. Edwin H. Cheney." The *Chicago Tribune,* which first broke the story of the couple's affair five years earlier, ran the details once again in a full-page spread.

In a rambling letter to the community, printed in the local newspapers, Wright paid tribute to his lost love: "She was true as only a woman who loves knows the meaning of the word. Her soul has entered me and it shall not be lost."

He praised the local residents for their acceptance of the couple: "No community anywhere could have received the trying circumstances of [Mamah's] life among you in a more high-minded way. I believe at no time has anything been shown her as she moved in your midst but courtesy and sympathy."

Wright devoted much of the statement to defending their relationship and attacking the newspapers for "the pestilential touch of stories made by the press for the man in the street." He went as far as comparing the *Chicago Tribune* to the murderous servant, writing that Carlton "struck in the heat of madness" while the *Tribune* "strikes the living and the dead in cool malice."

Wright continued:

> *Only true love is free love—no other kind is or ever can be free. The 'freedom' in which we joined was infinitely more difficult than any conformity with customs could have been. Few will ever venture it. It is not lives lived*

*on this plane that menace the well-being of society. No,
they can only serve to ennoble it.*

*You wives with your certificates for loving—pray that
you may love as much and be loved as well as was
Mamah Borthwick!*

Wright concluded by vowing to rebuild Taliesin. "I shall set it all
up again for the spirit of the mortals that lived in it and loved it—
will live in it still. My home will still be there."

Rebuild he did. But Taliesin II, as he called it, was destroyed by
fire in 1924, likely ignited by lightning. Taliesin's third incarnation
would be Wright's seasonal home and studio for the rest of his life.
Another studio, Taliesin West in Scottsdale, Arizona, was built as his
winter home in 1937.

Martha Borthwick was buried in the Wright family plot near Taliesin. Frank Lloyd Wright joined her after his death in 1959 at age
ninety-one. Upon the death of his third wife in 1985, Wright's
remains were cremated and moved to Taliesin West.

CARL'S SLED

- 1924 -

NORTHERN WISCONSIN WINTERS ARE THE STUFF OF LEGEND, an almost mythic backdrop for stories of men battling the elements, of awe-inspiring beauty, of ingenuity laughing in the face of crushing solitude. And in at least one case, of a guy who just wanted to go hunting in the snow.

In the middle of one Wisconsin winter nearly a century ago, Carl Eliason was working in the garage behind his family's general store in Saynor, Wisconsin, a venison-belt crossroads about fifteen miles south of Michigan's upper peninsula. Surrounded by small engine parts, hunting and fishing equipment, skis and snowshoes, and enough tools to open a hardware store, Eliason happily tinkered away in his cluttered workshop garage.

Carl Eliason loved to hunt and fish and trap as much as the next guy in Vilas County, but a bum foot had denied him the ability to make arduous treks through deep snow. For all practical purposes he was snowbound. Trying to solve the problem, he had once retooled a

Model T Ford with snow skis, but it didn't travel very well. His brother-in-law tried a wind-propelled machine, but that didn't quite make the grade either.

Eliason wasn't the only one trying to beat Wisconsin winters with modern machinery. Jury-rigged "snow buggies" were prevalent in these parts, even before 1900. Typical contraptions included bicycles with skis, steam-powered sleighs, and Model T Fords with runners mounted on the front. It was January when Eliason hammered two skis, a small boat engine, and some spare bicycle parts onto a toboggan. A couple of upgrades later, the young inventor thought his motorized sled worked well enough to file a patent.

He called his machine the Eliason Motor Toboggan. It used a 2.5 horsepower outboard engine, a continuous track made from bike sprockets and chains, and four skis, the front two controlled by a rope.

You can guess the rest of this only-in-America, necessity-is-the-mother-of-invention, right-time-right-place story.

Eliason personally produced forty toboggans during the next fifteen years. No more than three of his models were alike. Eventually, his four-cylinder "Frigid Flyer" could seat four people and reach speeds up to seventy miles per hour. By 1939, Carl's success was about to spark a mass production of his winter machines. Finland wanted two hundred models. The U.S. Army purchased 150 for use in the defense of Alaska during World War II. A group of Russians visited to test-drive the toboggans on the Pigeon River. (They borrowed a machine gun from the local library, mounted it on the hood, and fired imaginary bullets up and down the riverbank.)

To meet the challenge of mass production, Carl assigned his patents to the Four Wheel Drive Auto Company (FWD) of Clintonville, Wisconsin. He received royalties on all machines sold, and the company marketed the product worldwide under the Eliason name. The Model A, constructed with a twenty-five horsepower engine in 1940, was the first known factory-produced, single-track motor toboggan. It retailed for $525.

The 1940s also marked the beginning of the end for the "motor toboggan" name. "For advertising and convenience in handling," wrote the president of Four Wheel Drive, "we believe that the snowmobile would be a more appropriate name than the motor toboggan. This would give us a chance to expand the market for every type of conveyance off from the highway."

In other words, "snowmobile" fit better on a billboard.

Carl Eliason's original blueprint is unmistakable to this day, and motor tobogganing has become a new recreation, a new industry, a new way of life.

Wisconsin is not only the birthplace of the snowmobile; the Badger State has also become a snow-covered Oz encompassing twenty-five thousand miles of trails, the most extensive system in the nation. That's the equivalent of riding from Madison to Seattle and back . . . five times. Wisconsin trail number thirteen (there are forty-four others) traverses the state from north to south, making it possible to leave the Bucksnort Cafe in Land O'Lakes, on the Wisconsin/Michigan border, and arrive at Big Dog's Tap & Bowl in Sharon, on the Illinois border.

At the Amoco in Eagle River, motorists have to wait in line behind sleds before getting their own tanks topped off.

At the Honey Bear in St. Germain, the parking lot is filled for the Friday night fish fry not with SUVs or pickup trucks but with Ski-Doos and Arctic Cats.

In Eagle River, just down the road from Eliason Hardware in Saynor (where some of Carl's first models are displayed inside the store owned by Carl's grandson), you can find the Valvoline World Snowmobile Derby. More than thirty thousand people stand in the frigid weather to watch men and machines race at speeds exceeding one hundred miles per hour. It's the Daytona 500 of snowmobiling.

In St. Germain—a few miles or so down the road from Saynor—you can visit the Snowmobile Hall of Fame, "dedicated to preserving and showcasing the rich and exciting history of snowmobiling at both the recreational and competitive levels through the operation of a museum, hall of fame and library for the sport." That's a fancy way of saying come and look at twenty-five cool racing sleds, plus a lot of historic photos, trophies, and other memorabilia.

North of Highway 29, the words WELCOME SNOWMOBILERS appear on the marquee of most every lodging establishment, restaurant, and tavern.

It's sublime.

And all because Carl Eliason wanted to beat his buddies to the best ice-fishing hole.

Some of Eliason's original toboggans can be viewed at the Vilas County Historical Museum in Saynor. The museum is open every day in the summer; otherwise, stop by Eliason Hardware to see some of the early models.

Carl never reaped much profit on his invention. He made about $4,500 during his twenty-three-year partnership with FWD. His reward, it is said, came from watching the endless stream of snowmobilers ride past his office window along a major North Woods trail.

Carl Eliason died December 26, 1978. His funeral procession through Saynor was made, fittingly, on snowmobiles.

COOL CAL CHILLED IN SUPERIOR

- 1928 -

IT WAS JUST ANOTHER DAY IN THE NATION'S SEAT of power . . . presidential motorcades zipping back and forth; grim-faced secret service men staring down honest citizens; White House aides running around in circles; dark-suited dignitaries coming and going. But not the type of business you would typically find within the pastoral confines of Wisconsin.

During the summer of 1928, Superior Central High School played the role of the White House. Yes, *that* White House, the president's home, albeit minus the Lincoln Bedroom.

It was quite an honor for Superior, no doubt, but it's the Brule River that can take the credit. Seems we once had a president who had a genius for "effectively doing nothing." Except fishing. And he did that well all summer long on the Brule River.

After Calvin "Silent Cal" Coolidge took over following the death of Warren Harding, the presidential tradition of summer-long vacations came to include seasonal stays in the Adirondacks, the Black

Hills of South Dakota, and Swampscott, Massachusetts. At a time when the leader of the free world traditionally took the summer off, Coolidge excelled in at least this one arena.

Knowing the president had a serious jones for angling, Wisconsin senator Irvine Lenroot extended an open invitation to visit the Brule River. There was precedent, after all. Lenroot, from northern Wisconsin, had once entertained Warren Harding in his fishing lodge on the Brule. (In fact, Lenroot had almost become Harding's vice president, and would have succeeded him instead of Coolidge in 1923!)

On May 31, 1928, newspapers across the state screamed the news that Coolidge would spend his summer in Wisconsin. "The news was bombshelled onto the streets of Superior by an extra edition that violated all local newspaper rules and used a type four inches high for headlines," according to the *Wisconsin State Journal*.

In mid-June the president's train made its way through the state toward northern Wisconsin, but not without a little controversy. True to his taciturn form, Coolidge wasn't interested in greeting crowds waiting along the way. "1,000 Madisonians Fail to See Cal," snipped the *Wisconsin State Journal*. "For the second time in one year, Pres. Calvin Coolidge passed up Madison like a box car passes up a tramp."

"There were jeers, whistling, and then someone started the cry: 'We nominate Al Smith,'" the *State Journal* reported.

"The President, it appears, was not to be gaped at by the citizenry," the *Milwaukee Journal* added.

Servants stood in train vestibules and waved to the crowds in what must have been no consolation for the onlookers whatsoever.

Coolidge was certainly living up to his "Cool Cal" and "Silent Cal" nicknames. In another non-event during the train trip, Herbert Hoover was nominated by Republicans to succeed Coolidge, and reporters asked the president if he had any comment.

Nah.

The train rolled into Superior the morning of June 15. The streets were teeming with excited locals and spectators. Superior Central High School, dubbed the "northern White House," was headquarters for sixty soldiers, ten secret service men, fourteen servants, and seventy-five newsmen.

Coolidge did appear on the train platform this time. He waved his hat.

The real action, at least the only action Coolidge was concerned with, was on the Brule River. He jumped in a waiting convertible and left town, waving goodbye to the fifty thousand spectators along the way.

The president and first lady stayed not at the northern White House but at an estate built by oil baron H. C. Pierce some thirty miles away. Known as Cedar Island, the property contained 4,200 acres of the only remaining virgin forest in the state . . . and its very own trout hatchery.

"Imagine a cold, crystal-clear river loitering over golden sands and tumbling along pebbly rapids, stretching long loops through a wide green valley where tall Norway and white pines blanket the bends with deep shade making its way to a great inland sea that is never without a cool crisp breeze," rhapsodized one newspaper article in a painful example of how there was absolutely nothing of substance to report.

In a letter to her daughter-in-law, Mrs. Coolidge described the Brule River. "I cannot picture a more quiet scene than the one which lies before me as I sit on the porch of Cedar Island Lodge and look out upon it. Just here the Brule is a very quiet little stream. . . . The splash of the fish jumping is the only sound we have from it here. All was so quiet that when we first came I felt rather oppressed by it but once accustomed to it I do not mind and it certainly is peaceful and restful."

Good thing they became accustomed to the quiet. Cal was a lame duck. The president who effectively did nothing, according to contemporaries, was doing even more of that as his term wound down.

Mere hours after arriving at the lodge, Coolidge landed his first trout.

The next day he went fishing again. And the next. And the next. Pretty much every day for eighty-eight days. And he always wore a suit under his waders.

On July 5, the governor visited the president. They fished. One day Herbert Hoover stopped by. They fished. The head of the University of Wisconsin paid a visit. Coolidge fished after he left.

On Sundays the first couple would attend church at a country chapel where a blind pastor presided. Mrs. Coolidge said it took her back to her good old Methodist days.

Superior Central High School served as the official White House the whole time, though Coolidge rarely stopped in, and then only for perfunctory visits.

All in all, Wisconsin got an up close and personal view of a somewhat impersonal chief executive who demonstrated that his primary business was fishing.

When he and his wife left, Coolidge predicted that northern Wisconsin was "going to be a coming region for those who are seeking recreation."

He added, "The fishing around here, I can testify, is excellent."

THE STATE THAT MADE
PROHIBITION INFAMOUS

- 1929 -

A FEDERAL STUDY OF ALCOHOL ONCE CALLED Wisconsin the "Gibraltar of the wets—sort of a Utopia where everyone drinks their fill and
John Barleycorn still holds forth in splendor." Only problem with
that distinction is that it came during Prohibition when alcohol was
supposed to be illegal.

Chicago, with its vast underworld of big crime syndicates and
tommy gun shootists, may have put the roar in the Roaring Twenties,
but it was Wisconsin, with its steady resistance from otherwise law-
abiding citizens, that was a straw on the camel's back of Prohibition.
When temperance became the law of the land, Wisconsin virtually
seceded from the Union.

Even in 1929, ten years after the Eighteenth Amendment tried to
close the taps, things were not going well for Wisconsin's "dry" advo-
cates. The state's voters had just overwhelmingly approved a referen-
dum calling for an end to prosecutions related to alcohol violations.

Frank Buckley, a local agent with the Federal Bureau of Prohibition, declared the law "a catastrophe" that broke the "dikes of State cooperation [and] cleared the way for an even greater flood of intoxicants." He went on to add, "Liquor has always been plentiful in Wisconsin."

In completing his study of alcohol enforcement in Wisconsin, Buckley rated each county on a scale ranging from "dry" and "moist" to "wet" and "very wet." Forty-two of seventy-two counties were wet or worse.

"Most towns and cities throughout the state contain their allotment of soft-drink parlors," Buckley wrote. Beer, whiskey, and "shine" were available at every one. Sheriffs openly refused to enforce the law, and district attorneys did not bother prosecuting. Police were known to sample a refreshment or two themselves.

Tavern owners in Superior simply paid fines in the same manner as parking tickets. "The line formed on the right," Buckley reported. "The proprietor would reach into his pocket, extract therefrom a roll of bills, plead guilty, and place $200 on the desk."

In Brown County federal agents had to take matters into their own hands, padlocking forty-nine Green Bay taverns. "Conditions in this municipality are likewise unsatisfactory," reported Buckley. "The district attorney there, a star professional football player, devotes most of his efforts to that pastime." The sheriff was not much use either. The report noted that Green Bay's soft-drink parlors were prohibited from having curtains on the windows so the activities inside were open to plain view, but tavern owners simply pointed bright lights outward through the windows and let the glare do the rest.

Manitowoc and Outagamie contained "wildcat breweries," which supplied the local population as well as at least three other states. In Outagamie, a deputy sheriff helped identify federal agents as they entered the county, then notified the usual suspects.

Things were bleak in Juneau County, where the district attorney was slain by the ex-sheriff. "Both involved in liquor ring," the report stated.

And what about Milwaukee, home of the beverage that made the city famous? Buckley summed things up in three words: "All assistance needed." The 1,217 soft-drink parlors in the telephone book "all sell liquor."

Sheboygan County was "very wet" and rife with prostitution and gambling. The sheriff and district attorney passed the buck to one another.

And then there was Iron County, home of Hurley, the hardscrabble town made infamous by lumberjacks and miners, its condition described by Buckley as "general lawlessness." Hurley was "the worst community in the state. . . . Gambling, prostitution, bootlegging, and dope are about the chief occupations of the place. Saloons there function with barmaids who serve the dual capacity of soda dispenser and prostitute."

It wasn't always this way in Wisconsin. The first territorial settlers were Yankees with a strong reformist bent. They supported the abolition of slavery, suffrage for women, and temperance. "Drinking was one of many subjects," wrote Alice B. Smith in the *History of Wisconsin, Volume 1,* "on which native and foreigner totally failed to reach an understanding . . . the devotion of Irishmen to whiskey and Germans to beer was regarded as total depravity."

In 1848, twelve breweries opened in Wisconsin. By 1860 there were nearly two hundred churning out their products. Milwaukee alone had forty.

When Chicago suffered the ravages of its devastating 1871 fire, the Schlitz Brewery, located nearby across the Illinois/Wisconsin border, saw a 100 percent jump in sales and became known as "the beer that made Milwaukee famous."

Wisconsin brewers went nationwide. Milwaukee beer baron Captain Fred Pabst bought property in New York City, including a part of Times Square, and opened wildly successful beer gardens. He pioneered another trend by devoting considerable budgets to mass advertising. Miller, Schlitz, and G. Heileman in La Crosse soon followed suit.

In the most German state in the nation, brewing stood among the region's top industries. Every town had a brewery. Indeed, some towns formed because of breweries. Milwaukee had 3,500 taverns. La Crosse's five breweries directly or indirectly employed more than 1,600 people, paying millions in salaries and taxes.

The golden age of the golden drink was on.

Places like the Schlitz Palm Garden, one article reminisced, "had no duplicate in the United States. Only in Europe, possibly only in Germany, could similar halls be found, where members of the family, from grandpa to the babe in arms might be found—in the old days—listening to the concert, while adults sipped beer. It was one of the show places—for some years the principal one—of Milwaukee."

But then came Prohibition, and Wisconsin's slow, stubborn assault on the notion of temperance. Wisconsin voters made their sentiments clear when they elected Governor John J. Blaine to the United States Senate. His platform was brilliantly straightforward: "Bring Back Beer." The repeal of Prohibition was introduced to Congress in February of 1933, approved by the Senate two days later, and ratified on December 5, 1933, as the Twenty-first Amendment. National prohibition ended in time for the holidays.

Wisconsin no doubt celebrated as you might expect from a place previously called "the Gibraltar of the wets," but the morning after may have felt a bit worse by the knowledge that the gilded age of Wisconsin's brewing industry was gone forever, as most breweries did not survive the great social experiment known as Prohibition.

SMILING JOE

- 1930 -

BOXING WAS INTRODUCED AT MARQUETTE UNIVERSITY in the fall of 1930. Among the five thousand students attending the Milwaukee school, one freshman pugilist began receiving special attention. The *Marquette Tribune* called him a "husky, hard-hitting middleweight who promises an evening's work for any foe."

According to his sparring partner, the freshman was slow and a wild puncher, but the kid loved to brawl, and he was absolutely fearless. In turn, he struck fear in his opponents, tearing into his rivals with a flurry of punches, never bothering with a strategy or a defense. If an opponent landed a punch, it was returned twice as hard. In one match, a crowd of nine hundred watched "Smiling Joe," as the student newspaper called him, send a bigger man to the canvas three times in the first round.

By the spring of 1931, Smiling Joe was aiming bigger, challenging a heavyweight named Stan Balcerzak. Joe lost in a decision before 3,500 spectators. Undaunted, he requested a rematch; the second time around he sent Balcerzak to the canvas for a nine-count and ended up winning in a decision.

Toward the end of his second year of boxing at Marquette, Smiling Joe stopped by the local Eagles Club, where he occasionally sparred with the locals. He told the boxing instructor he was going to turn professional.

"Stay in college," he was told flatly. The instructor, a man named Fred Saddy, said he would trade the heavyweight title itself for a university diploma.

The young man took Saddy's advice to heart, turning his attention to the next most bruising profession he could imagine after boxing. Law.

From the very start, "Smiling Joe" McCarthy, the fearless middleweight from Appleton, had a taste for the jugular.

In his third year at Marquette, McCarthy joined a legal fraternity, Delta Theta Phi, and the Franklin Debating Club, where he thrived on the verbal jousting matches. Not that he was all that good. His speeches were thrown together at the last minute, and they typically contained exaggerations to cover his lack of preparation. Instead of logic and reasoning, McCarthy attacked his opponents with verbal abuse on a par with his boxing style.

"Then, very quickly," wrote one biographer, "he would forget the entire encounter and commence buying Cokes, slapping people on the back, and swapping jokes. Nobody could stay angry at Joe McCarthy. He wouldn't let you."

More than seventy-five years since his college days and nearly fifty since his death, Joe McCarthy's name remains familiar to America. Few other "isms" in western history come close to the one attached to his name, and the controversies he inflamed burn to this very day.

He was Wisconsin's United States senator, twice elected, and he defeated Bob La Follette Jr., son of perhaps Wisconsin's greatest politician. His reelection came not long before he was disgraced as a modern-day witch hunter.

How in the world did a state known for its progressive political heritage send to the United States Senate a frustrated amateur boxer who became the very definition of demagogue?

With the benefit of hindsight, McCarthy's Marquette years tell us all we need to know. Underlying the familiar personality traits that would contribute to the rise and fall of Joe McCarthy—recklessness, verbal abusiveness, and exaggerations—he also had about him a personable charm. He was "a lovable sort of guy," as one of his teachers explained.

"His face would beam when you met him," said one of his fraternity brothers. "I don't think he had an enemy in the class."

"The hilarity seemed to intensify as soon as he walked through the door," wrote biographer Thomas C. Reeves. "He drank beer (a few glasses were his limit), told stories, played tricks, kidded everyone in sight, and gambled recklessly."

Throughout his life, those who knew or met McCarthy could not deny his affability. "Almost all of the scores of people who labored for the election of Joe McCarthy," wrote Reeves, "were primarily attracted to his personality . . . the flow of energy, friendliness and self-confidence that radiated from the youthful campaigner."

His reserves of energy and outgoing personality made for a potent political alchemy. The hyperactive young McCarthy didn't just campaign in communities across Wisconsin, he stormed them, and when he had finished working his way through a dozen towns in a typical eighteen-hour campaign day, everybody knew "Joe."

Some of his closest supporters came from his Marquette days. In the fall of 1933, the father of one of McCarthy's classmates died unexpectedly. McCarthy rushed to the student's rooming house and quickly made train arrangements for the grieving young man. Then he borrowed a Model T Ford and made the arduous round-trip drive between Milwaukee and Mauston to attend the services. Twenty years later, when McCarthy was under siege, the classmate would tell a reporter, "He cut classes, left his job, and borrowed money to get there. He did that for me, and he'll always be my friend."

Everybody had a story like that. Joe milking cows for farmers, Joe washing dishes for the housewives, Joe handing out lollipops to the girls.

McCarthy had picked up another preoccupation while at Marquette: he loved poker. Not that he was any good. Sometimes he would make bets before looking at the hand. To compensate, he became a master at bluffing, playing up the country boy bit then upping the ante to force his opponents out of the game. "He bluffed so much that his opponents could never tell whether he had a good hand or a bad one," according to one contemporary. It was an act he played time and again throughout his life, both in high-stakes poker games and high-stakes politics. When in doubt, bluff. Fake it.

Near the end of his first term, McCarthy needed an issue that could generate some headlines and help get him reelected. The notion of playing on the nation's anti-Communist anxiety must have seemed like a good idea. In 1950, he made a speech in Wheeling, West Virginia, claiming that he was holding in his hand a list of state department employees who were known members of the Communist Party. But the response following his 1950 speech alleging Communism in the federal government surprised even McCarthy.

It all caught up with him of course—the reckless political attacks, the incessant verbal abuse of Senate witnesses, bluffing time and again to cover his own exaggerations. Two years after being reelected in 1952, the Senate censured McCarthy for smearing committee witnesses as Communists (he had precious little or no evidence), only the fourth senator in United States history to be so reprimanded.

Even more than gambling, another vice, drinking (which had perhaps contributed to his boorish behavior during the famous Senate hearings), took hold. Bitter, alcoholic, and paranoid, when the senator died in 1957, little remained of the original "Smiling Joe" who had won over so many Wisconsin voters with his infectious energy and common touch. His greatest attribute, the legendary McCarthy charm, was gone. Nevertheless, at his funeral in Appleton, more than thirty thousand people filed through the church to pay their respects.

His papers were given to his alma mater. Among the many speeches contained in the Joseph R. McCarthy Papers at Marquette University is a 1950 address he delivered in Milwaukee. The occasion was a tribute dinner for Fred Saddy, the former Eagles Club boxing trainer who had become head of the National Boxing Association. With a warm smile McCarthy spoke fondly of Saddy and the Marquette days. He recounted the story, as he had done many times over the years, about how his life would have taken a different course if not for the sound advice of the boxing instructor.

Our world, too, would have taken a different course had Joe McCarthy chosen boxing over politics.

VALLEY OF THE MOLLS

- 1934 -

IT WASN'T ALL THAT UNUSUAL TO SEE SEDANS WITH Illinois plates paying a visit to northern Wisconsin's secluded lodges, but something
about this new group looked suspicious. The tourist season was still
more than a month away for one thing, and ice was still on the lakes.
And this group that had just arrived at the Little Bohemia Lodge in
Manitowish Waters, with their dark suits and somber expressions,
obviously weren't interested in the fishing.

The lodge owner, Emil Wanatka, noted how the men's suits
bulged under their arms, a fashion statement that came from pack-
ing .45 pistols in shoulder holsters. Turns out, the man in charge of
the group was none other than John Dillinger. Accompanying him
were Homer Van Meter, John "Three Fingered Jack" Hamilton,
Tommy Carroll, and the killer's killer himself, Lester Gillis, aka
"Baby Face Nelson."

After a few tense days at the hands of their benevolent-yet-scary
guests, Wanatka's wife couldn't take it anymore. She made a daring

trip into town and smuggled messages written in matchbooks to relatives who contacted the feds in Chicago.

On April 22, 1934, dozens of government agents converged on Little Bohemia. Freezing cold and nervous, agents mistakenly opened fire on three Civilian Conservation Corps workers as they were leaving the lodge bar, killing one of them and injuring the others. Alerted by the shooting, the gang returned the agents' fire, bolted through the back windows . . . and disappeared into the woods.

The violent shootout and miraculous escape would be immortalized time and again in books, magazines, movies, and television.

Generally forgotten is that ten hours later, the agents were still shooting at Little Bohemia, believing they had the gang cornered.

A voice came from the basement: "We'll come out if you stop firing."

The desperate cries of desperate men it was not. Emerging from Little Bohemia through the early morning haze and tear gas were three young women abandoned by the gang, two of them dressed in pajamas and another holding a Boston bull terrier named Rex.

Virtually everyone in the nation was fixated by Dillinger's daring escape. President Roosevelt addressed the nation and spurred Congress to pass a number of anticrime bills. As director of the Bureau of Investigation, J. Edgar Hoover issued a "shoot to kill" order. The largest manhunt in history fanned out through five states.

Wisconsin may have been home to both Manitowish Waters and Madison, but the state's remote North Woods and the downstate capital city were worlds apart, separated by a five-hour drive along Highway 51. There was nothing about the shootout way "up there" to get excited about in the sophisticated government and university town.

Until the gang girls arrived.

"Dillinger gang molls behind bars here," announced the *Wisconsin State Journal*, igniting a pandemonium that would plague the city for weeks. The murderous outlaws, it was commonly accepted, would surely spring their female companions from jail.

Sheriff Fred Finn, fearing an assault on his jail, immediately set a lethal trap of bait and switch. The gang would be greeted by a shower of bullets if they tried to fight their way in, while the women would be hidden somewhere else in the city.

But where?

Finn smuggled his three prisoners into the last place John Dillinger would ever be caught dead: St. Raphael's Catholic Church, just across the street from the jail. The women made their beds on the hard oak pews.

Federal agents descended on Madison. The *Capital Times* reported, "A picked squad of the best sharpshooters in the department of justice was speeding to Wisconsin as the government net was drawing closer on the fleeing gang chieftain and his aides."

The day after the women arrived in town, a bulletin confirmed Madison's worst fears. "Men believed to be John Dillinger and three henchmen were reported heading in the direction of Madison at 8 o'clock this morning. In Milwaukee, four men armed with machine guns were sighted in a big car speeding out of the city along Highway 18," reported the *Milwaukee Journal.*

The city became a virtual police state. Federal agents hit the streets in "heavily armed" vehicles. Madison police stopped dark sedans at random. Armed guards walked Sheriff Finn's kids to school.

At noon, a salesman reported seeing three "roughly dressed" men at a crossroads northwest of the city. Agents and county deputies moved into position, girding their loins for a do-or-die battle with the most notorious gang in the nation's history.

A six-hour search, however, produced no "roughly dressed" men. The *London Times* reported that in the Wild West of Wisconsin "even some red Indians joined the hunt today with bows and arrows."

In Washington, the attorney general asked for airplanes, armored cars, and additional men to catch Dillinger. If the FBI had had an armored car at Little Bohemia, "this terrible tragedy would not have happened."

Similarly, the Madison Common Council moved quickly, albeit quietly, to transfer funds to the police department. The council had previously balked at the police department's request for a machine gun. Now the council hoped to make the appropriation in secret—until the *Capital Times* reported on its front page that two thousand dollars would be invested in a machine gun, bullets, a bulletproof vest, and an armored car.

In the center of the fear and the frenzy and the shotguns remained the women. Authorities struggled to determine their identity. One maintained she was Ann Sothern, a popular actress of the day.

According to the United Press, as the agents interrogated the women, "valuable information regarding John Dillinger and his gang slipped from the lips of their three deserted feminine consorts today. Bit by bit the gangsters' girls offered information, bargaining for sleep and rest."

A woman who had given her name as Marion Marr told agents that she had been married only two weeks to one of the gangsters. "Gangster's Bride Spends Honeymoon Alone in Cell," read the headline in the *Wisconsin State Journal*. "County Jail is Honeymoon Hotel to Gangster Girl," echoed the *Capital Times*. Marion Marr, it was later discovered, turned out to be Helen Gillis, wife of Baby Face Nelson. She had been married to the killer for six years and was a mother of two children whose whereabouts were unknown.

The woman going by the name of Ann Sothern then said her real name was Ann Delaney. Her attorney informed the police that she was really Jean Compton.

"Rose Ancker" turned out to be one Marie Conforti.

The extent of the women's complicity with the gang remained a mystery. The prisoners admitted only one thing: they missed Rex, the dog.

After several weeks of hysteria, the women were given a suspended sentence for harboring a fugitive and were placed on probation.

"I don't think you are a bad girl," the Judge told Conforti. "I know you're not. You just got into some bad company." Turning to the crowded courtroom, he continued, "I am satisfied this mere girl had no knowledge these men were gangsters. I am convinced she would not have jeopardized her own life by associating with dangerous criminals."

After the proceedings, the *Wisconsin State Journal* asked the women how they enjoyed their stay in Madison.

Conforti: "I'm saying nothing."

Compton: "What I've seen of Madison, I don't like."

Gillis: "I hope I never see this state again."

Before catching a train to Chicago, the three women went shopping around the Capitol Square and enjoyed beer and potato salad at a drugstore. They changed their tune and praised Madison as a beautiful lake city full of "nice shops."

"Turn a woman loose, and she's bound to go shopping!" wrote the *Capital Times*. The items bought by the women "proved their excellent taste."

"We're not 'molls' or 'gang girls'" they told the reporter. "After we've reported to the probation judge in Chicago, we're going right out to look for jobs and start all over."

Still, questions lingered after the three women waved goodbye from the train depot. Were these gangster "molls"? Or good women keeping bad company?

Jean Compton reunited with Tommy Carroll and was with him when he was gunned down in Waterloo, Iowa, three weeks later.

Marie Conforti and Homer Van Meter were together when Van Meter was killed in a gunfight with St. Paul police in August.

Helen Gillis and Baby Face Nelson were spotted driving a stolen car near Barrington, Illinois, in November. In the ensuing gunfight, Baby Face killed two federal agents and was mortally wounded. Helen Gillis left her husband's body at a local cemetery. She was arrested two days later and sentenced to a year in prison for violating parole. Helen Gillis died in 1987.

IT HAPPENED IN NECEDAH, ALLEGEDLY

- 1950 -

MARY ANN VAN HOOF, A SLIGHT, PLAIN FARMWOMAN who resided with her husband and seven children near Necedah, awoke in her bed one night with a feeling that somebody was in the room. Standing before her was the Virgin Mary. She wore a cream-colored dress with a light blue cloak that had blue stars at the bottom. Despite a thin veil that covered the apparition's head, Van Hoof could see that Mary was a blonde.

Frightened, Van Hoof pulled the sheets over her head.

Five months later, on the evening of Good Friday, 1950, Van Hoof noticed that the crucifix on her wall was glowing. A voice said, "I will come again when the grass is green and the leaves are on the trees, but not in this room."

Van Hoof later said it was the most beautiful voice she had ever heard.

Indeed, on May 28, with the fields and trees in full bloom, Van Hoof stepped to the door of her humble farmhouse to call the kids to dinner. She saw a flash of light by the ash trees in the yard.

"I looked up and out through the door and saw a blue mist behind some trees, then the vision became the figure of our Mother," she said. "She was so radiant and beautiful an artist couldn't paint her to justice."

The apparition instructed her to build a shrine.

Obediently, Van Hoof erected a statue of the Virgin Mary in the middle of the four ash trees. Word soon spread around the town of 838 people that this was another Fatima (the town in Portugal made famous for the Marian visions said to have taken place in 1917). Members of the clergy, believers, and the simply curious began flocking to the shrine.

Initially the messages, as relayed through Van Hoof, were relatively simple. "Pray, pray, pray, pray hard," she told pilgrims.

The farm wife had been told to "bring the truth to all people." But the truth wasn't the only thing Van Hoof planned to bring to the people. She began selling "magic pillows," too.

The curious tale of Mary Ann "Annie" Van Hoof began with her mother, a Hungarian who had reputedly dabbled in spiritualism and witchcraft with Transylvanian gypsies. After settling in Kenosha, the mother-daughter duo held séances and began frequenting a spiritualist camp in Wonewoc.

Word of Van Hoof's visions soon reached the Catholic Diocese of La Crosse, which decided to take a look-see. Bishop John Treacy concluded that the claims were "spurious" and "highly questionable," the product of "unstable emotionalism and misguided zeal." He prohibited religious services at the site.

Undaunted, Van Hoof announced that another appearance would take place August 15, 1950, on the Catholic holy day known as the Assumption of the Blessed Virgin Mary.

Van Hoof was now generating headlines near and far. More than 175,000 copies of a pamphlet written by Necedah believers were circulated throughout the country. Anticipation mounted through the hot summer of 1950.

Extra trains and buses were arranged from points throughout the Midwest to accommodate demand leading up to the event. Pilgrims filled motels across Wisconsin. Others camped nearby.

Bishop Treacy did his best to stem the inexorable tide of people heading to Necedah. The woman's claims were "extremely doubtful in nature," he reiterated. "Stay at home and pray the rosary there."

By the morning of August 15, four vast farm fields were filled with as many as fifteen thousand parked cars. The roadways were choked with many more. Hundreds of buses had been chartered. Trains rolled into Necedah every twenty minutes. Media correspondents counted license plates from thirty-eight states. Planes circled overhead.

Just before noon, Van Hoof, her husband, children, and mother walked from the house and knelt at the shrine.

"An impressive hush fell over the throng," reported the *Necedah Republican*. The crowd was estimated at one hundred thousand people. "There was literally not a human sound."

Van Hoof prayed for ten minutes. Then she addressed the crowd at a microphone, repeating what she had just been told by the Blessed Virgin.

"All religions must work together, not in jealousy and hatred, but in love. Love thy neighbor. Love thy neighbor."

She spoke for about ten minutes before she was overcome with emotion and walked back into the house. A delegation from the La Crosse diocese followed her inside for questioning.

That was it.

Through the farmhouse screen door, reporters asked family members if Mary Ann had seen the Blessed Virgin.

"She says what a silly question," answered Van Hoof's daughter. "Yes."

Another "vision day," supposedly the last, was held in October. Radio broadcasts of the event were cancelled under pressure from the church. The crowd was significantly smaller, but thousands still came. This gathering was a bit more dramatic. As she held her crucifix aloft, the sun broke through the clouds, causing a stir in the crowd. Van Hoof repeated many of the same messages as before. Then she collapsed at the shrine, striking her head on the pedestal.

Van Hoof carried on for decades to come, allegedly suffering stigmata and seeing miniature angels and saints in trees and on fenceposts. Her messages became increasingly bizarre. She urged followers to sign up for a spaceship captained by an ancient man named Alex who would take true believers into the center of the earth after the Apocalypse. She claimed thirty thousand priests in the United States were Soviet spies.

A nonprofit group called For My God and My Country was established to maintain the shrine in 1958, and it still operates a K-12 school, Queen of the Holy Rosary Mediatrix of Peace.

The church drew a hard line: "All claims regarding supernatural revelations and visions made by Mrs. Van Hoof are false. Furthermore, all public and private religious worship connected with these false claims is prohibited." In the 1970s, the La Crosse diocese excommunicated anyone associated with the shrine. Van Hoof responded by creating an order of sisters who dressed like nuns and made up their own vows.

"Until her death in 1984," wrote religious scholar Kevin Orlin Johnson, "it was all Commie plots hatched by a Council of Elders, mind control through fluoridation, and global nuclear conflict that would destroy everything outside a thirty mile radius of Necedah, where a spaceship would come to take them to a paradise inside the hollow Earth."

Van Hoof's followers took on the characteristics of a cult. The women wore blue skirts to look "Marylike." They created their own flag. And they prepared for doomsday, which was always around the corner.

"It is well known that there's a certain survivalist mentality with regard to the shrine," said a diocese spokesman in 1998. "I think there are certain elements that are cultic in nature."

Today, a small group of families (known as "shriners" by locals) still live and believe in Van Hoof's Necedah proclamations, or "the cause," as they say.

But the days when tens of thousands made their pilgrimage to her farm are long gone, faded like the weather-beaten statues dotting the landscape.

A SUMMER IN EAU CLAIRE

- 1952 -

ON JUNE 20, 1952, A PROMISING YOUNG BASEBALL PLAYER named Henry Aaron, eighteen years old and just days into his minor-league career, took his place as shortstop for the Eau Claire Bears.

Aaron's debut a week earlier had been "auspicious," according to the *Eau Claire Leader*. He hit two singles on his first two times at bat, whetting the appetite of fans in this baseball-loving town in the Northern League.

The Bears were playing their rivals from Superior, the Blues, at Carson Park—Eau Claire's classic stadium.

It was the top of the eighth inning. Superior's Chuck Wiles, a catcher, was on first base. Wiles was an up-and-comer. He had been guaranteed a spring training spot in the majors the following season. For now he was helping lead Superior to first place.

With Wiles on base, the next Blues player stepped to the plate and hit a grounder. Second baseman Bob McConnell fielded the ball away from his base and flipped the ball to Aaron, who tagged second and wound up to make the double play with a throw to first.

Aaron's throwing style—sidearm, almost underhand—was unorthodox. He fired the ball low as Wiles was bearing down on second base.

The ball struck Wiles in the head a split second after leaving Aaron's hand. The sickening thud of impact echoed across the ballpark. The ball rebounded off of Wiles's right ear and rolled into right field.

"Wiles was carried from the field with a slight concussion," the *Leader* reported. "The injured catcher was expected to return with the team to Superior unless held at the hospital here for observation."

Wiles didn't leave the hospital for two weeks. He slipped into a coma for three days and was placed on the hospital's critical list.

"Aaron's throw destroyed Wiles's inner ear, altering his equilibrium and sense of balance," according to Jerry Poling in *A Summer Up North*. "He spent months learning to walk again. For several years he suffered from severe concussion headaches."

Eventually, Wiles had his inner ear removed. Not only was his career finished, Wiles was unable to work any job again and suffered small strokes likely related to the head trauma.

It was a tragic accident in the days before batting helmets—a time when it wasn't altogether uncommon to hear of young men dying from being struck in the head with a baseball.

For Aaron, it was a crossroads. He was a shy teenager far from home for the first time, a black kid all alone in a white man's world. He had the quiet confidence to make it in the pros, but that was all he had. Painfully lonely and deeply despondent over Wiles's injury, Aaron faced the first major decision in his young life.

He made up his mind and called home.

Henry Louis Aaron left his hometown of Mobile, Alabama, just shy of completing his senior year in high school. It was April 1952. He had been playing weekend shortstop for Mobile's semi-pro team, the Black Bears, and was sent to North Carolina to train with the Indianapolis Clowns, one of only six teams remaining with the dying Negro Leagues.

He carried with him two dollars and two sandwiches.

More than once Aaron reportedly thought about getting off the train and heading back to Mobile.

"He wasn't just any Eau Claire Bears player," wrote Poling. "He was supposed to be a phenom, one of the legion of young black players expected to follow on Jackie Robinson's heels and change baseball forever."

He was also a black kid who only knew life in the segregated South. Tiny Eau Claire, Wisconsin, was like another planet to Aaron. Other than two black teammates, he saw only one black person in Eau Claire that summer.

Then came the fateful moment against Superior when Wiles went down with a grotesque thud.

"I wasn't much of a talker anyway, but in Eau Claire you couldn't pry my mouth open," Aaron said later. "It didn't take much to tell that my way of talking was different than the way people talked in Wisconsin, and I felt freakish enough as it was."

Now, on top of it all, Aaron was deeply distraught. Fans of the Superior Blues made it worse by mercilessly taunting the young man. It broke him. He phoned his family in Mobile and said that he was coming home. He couldn't take it anymore.

Aaron's brother Herbert got on the phone. "Are you crazy?" Herbert demanded.

"He said there was nothing to come home to," Aaron recounted in his autobiography, "and if I left I'd be walking out on the best break I could ever hope to get."

With that, the harsh minor league trial-by-fire for Henry Aaron ended. So did his premature retirement.

Over the years, Aaron would hear countless stories from other black players who had also almost quit the minors.

Without missing a game, Henry Aaron returned to the line-up and lit up the Northern League, though the Bears fell short of the pennant. He was the runaway winner of the league's rookie-of-the-year honors.

The rest, as they say, is history.

Thirty years from that summer, on July 21, 1982, Henry "Hammering Hank" Aaron was inducted into the National Baseball Hall of Fame. When he returned to Eau Claire on August 17, 1994, to unveil a bust of himself at Carson Park, he was a national sports hero.

In 2002 he received the Presidential Medal of Freedom.

PSYCHO

- 1958 -

THE POLICE CAPTAIN DIDN'T KNOW WHERE TO START. He had written plenty of reports in his career, but nothing like this.

"It was eight P.M.," he began. "We tried the doors. They were locked but the door leading into a woodshed attached to the house didn't seem to be latched too tight. I put my foot against it and pushed and the door came open."

Knowing the suspect had no electricity, the captain and a deputy sheriff flicked on their service flashlights. They stepped inside the shed.

They were looking for Ed Gein, the odd little man who lived alone on this farm. A woman had been murdered, and police had suspected Gein immediately. A few years earlier, he'd been questioned in the disappearance of a female tavern owner.

The police captain was stepping from the shed to the house when he heard his partner cry out behind him, "My God, there she is."

"I went over to where he was and saw a woman's . . . body hanging from the rafters by her ankles. We then went into the house and found it to be in a terrible state, completely littered from one end of the house to the other with bones, barrels of junk, stacks of clothes, papers, and so forth."

They also found skulls, pieces of skin, and bones. Richard Hendricks in *Weird Wisconsin* wrote, "Ask any non-Wisconsinite to name the first things that come to mind about Wisconsin, and inevitably they are cheese, the Green Bay Packers, and Ed Gein—not necessarily in that order."

More than fifty years after he began robbing women's graves to create a bodysuit made of their remains, forty-some years since he was first immortalized in horror movies, and twenty years after he was buried in the same cemetery where his infamy began, Ed Gein remains the ghoul who keeps on giving.

The product of an overbearing, fanatically religious mother whom he adored, the peculiar Eddie began losing touch with reality not long after her death in 1945. He sealed her room exactly as it was and began indulging in robbing graves. He violated at least six gravesites in Plainfield, more in nearby communities, and went to work on a dress.

Over a period of ten years, Gein decorated his filthy farmhouse with his gruesome trophies. When grave robbing wasn't enough, Gein turned to murder, claiming his first victim, tavern keeper Mary Hogan, in 1954. A second victim, Plainfield hardware store owner Bernice Worden, was murdered three years later.

Worden's homicide led to Gein's arrest on November 16, 1957. Gein had stopped by Worden's hardware store in Plainfield earlier that day. Finding her alone in the store, Gein had retrieved a .22 rifle from his truck, told Worden he was interested in buying a new gun, and then shot her in the back of the head as she turned away. Worden's son discovered his mother missing later that afternoon and noticed a streak of blood leading out the back door. It was Bernice

Worden's body that officers had found in the woodshed that night. Gein was arrested at the grocery store in town about the same time that police were searching his farmhouse.

Reporters from all over the world flocked to central Wisconsin.

Plainfield is a small town. Everybody knew Eddie, the victims as well as the people whose graves he violated. There was a collective sense of trauma in Plainfield. Ed Gein was sent away for good, as you would expect, but the small town has never quite escaped him.

His farm became a morbid tourist site. The house was set to be auctioned, but before it could be sold, it was burned to the ground in a "mysterious" fire.

Still, the morbid curiosity about Gein continues to ebb and flow.

In 1960, Alfred Hitchcock filmed a movie based loosely on Gein. You know the name. *Psycho.* Another movie with elements of Gein written all over it, *Silence of the Lambs,* was a blockbuster in 1991.

Ed Gein jokes—"Geiners"—once rampant in schoolyards and taverns across the land, can still occasionally be heard.

Gein died at the Mendota Mental Health Institute in Madison, on July 26, 1984. The obituary appeared in newspapers around the world.

As if another wave of attention wasn't enough for folks in Plainfield, Eddie was returned to the local cemetery and buried next to his beloved mother. Thrill seekers beat a path to his gravesite and Gein's tombstone soon became chipped and defaced by the visitors. Authorities grew tired of flushing teens from the cemetery late at night. In June 2000 the tombstone was stolen. It was discovered soon after in Seattle, where rubbings were being sold for $50. The marker now resides in a Waushara County museum.

In 2006 the man who owns Gein's forty acres of farmland in Waushara County posted the property for sale on eBay, the online merchandiser. The asking price was $250,000—at least twice as much as any other forty-acre spread in the area. "Ed Gein's Farm . . . The REAL Deal!" received heavy Internet traffic and a fair amount of media attention before the ad was pulled. A victims' rights group had complained about using Gein's infamy to inflate the price. A group spokesman said the Gein land was "the highest ticket item in the murder memorabilia racket" since they started watchdogging items in 1999.

And so it goes. Little Plainfield, and to an extent Wisconsin, can't escape the curse.

THE MAKING OF A PRESIDENT'S BABY

- 1960 -

DURING THE WINTER OF 1960, Massachusetts senator John F. Kennedy and Minnesota senator Hubert H. Humphrey waged a tight battle for the Democratic presidential nomination. Wisconsin was an early primary state and boneyard for many a struggling presidential candidate. Humphrey, heavily favored due to his Midwest roots, was pressing Kennedy to schedule a debate, something the Kennedy campaign embraced with all the enthusiasm of lukewarm chowder.

The campaigns played a game of cat and mouse in the Badger State, especially in the third congressional district—the key battleground along the state's western border.

According to the *Boscobel Dial:*

> *Hard on the heels of Sen. Humphrey was Sen. John*
> *Kennedy of Massachusetts, whose caravan followed*
> *Humphrey's through the hills of southwestern Wisconsin*
> *Friday but studiously avoided a meeting. Kennedy had*

a small crowd in Boscobel as local Democrats who made arrangements for Humphrey were not fully prepared for Kennedy. The 42-year-old easterner dropped in at the Dial *office and had his picture taken. He also ducked in downtown stores to shake a few hands. In Meller's Drug Store Kennedy rearranged a magazine shelf to put a magazine with his picture on the cover in better view.*

Traveling with the caravan was Jacqueline Kennedy. (According to former *Dial* owner Ralph Goldsmith, the future first lady acted more than a little aloof when asked if she enjoyed rural Wisconsin.)

That afternoon, Senator and Mrs. Kennedy rested in room nineteen of the Boscobel Hotel. This particular room in the hotel already had a history. One night in 1898, two traveling salesmen sat in the room and brainstormed about an organization that would fortify fellow travelers with the Good Word. Since then, "the Gideons" have distributed tens of millions of Bibles worldwide.

When the Kennedys stopped at the hotel for their afternoon rest, they were given the most famous room in the house, even though it was smaller than one of Jackie's walk-in closets.

Here's the kicker: local legend says that the resting part came only after John Jr. was conceived. Of course nobody knows for certain, but the campaign visit and the folklore associated with it are an integral part of the considerable history of this river city hotel.

The Kennedy campaign stop at the Boscobel Hotel occurred on March 25, 1960. John-John was born on November 25, approximately eight months later. So it's maybe, er, conceivable.

Problem is, the future president and his wife spent so much time campaigning in Wisconsin during the cold winter of 1960 that any establishment with a room could make the same claim. From January 21, 1960, when Kennedy announced his candidacy in the Wisconsin primary, to April 5, the primary election date, the Kennedy couple practically took up residency in the Badger State. The Buckhorn Bar in Spooner still displays a plaque on the men's room door: JOHN F. KENNEDY USED THESE FACILITIES on March 18, 1960.

Approximately nine months before John-John's birth, the Kennedys visited Menomonie. The candidate spoke at Harvey Hall on the University of Wisconsin–Stout campus and made a pit stop at, you guessed it, the local Hotel Marion.

Even two Kennedy aides, Kenneth O' Donnell and Dave Powers, had some fun with the conception speculation in their 1973 book, *Johnny We Hardly Knew Ye*:

> *When we arrived in Fort Atkinson, a town noted for manufacturing sausages and musical saws, the wife of the local Lutheran minister was waiting outside the Blackhawk Hotel with her thirteen children, eager to introduce them to the Senator . . . Jack shook hands with the beaming mother and each of her children, posed for pictures with them, and then said to me, "Get Jackie and bring her over here." . . . Jack introduced her to the mother of thirteen children and said to her, "Shake hands with this lady, Jackie. Maybe it will rub off on you."*

"That was on February 15, 1960," wrote Powers. "Nine months later John F. Kennedy, Junior, was born."

As far as we know, John Jr. never shared this sort of family information, even when he made an occasional visit to Wisconsin. We do know, however, that on August 21, 1995, he ate an "omelette w/ extra items, Buttrmlk Pcks w/meat, large juice" before kayaking around the Apostle Islands. (The restaurant at Greunke's Inn, Bayfield, has the bill framed for posterity.)

Back in Boscobel, where it's always 1960, one alternative scenario is that Kennedy needed time to prepare for the major foreign policy speech delivered later that night at the University of Wisconsin Field House in Madison. When he appeared following a hotel stop, the *Wisconsin State Journal* reported that despite his grueling schedule, the candidate looked "refreshed."

Draw your own conclusions.

OUR WOOLLIES CHANGED HISTORY

- 1964 -

IT STARTED OUT AS A TYPICAL DAY ON Frank Schaefer's Kenosha farm in 1964. Fields to be plowed, soybeans to be planted, human history to be rewritten.

Frank was plowing a field, unhappy about whatever it was—a rock, probably—that broke a blade on his tiller. He turned off the engine and climbed down to take a look. Hidden in the topsoil was not a rock, but a bone. Considerably larger than a bone from your average dog, deer, or old pioneer.

Schaefer called the local museum, thinking they might be interested. The museum didn't have the staff or resources to look, they explained, but maybe the caller could find an amateur archaeologist. Schaefer had a man named Phil Sander draw a sketch map of where the artifact was found, then he donated the bone to the museum.

Turns out the bone was from a woolly mammoth, the hairy, long-tusked beasts that roamed the earth during the Ice Age. But the museum already possessed mammoth bones discovered locally in the

1920s and 1930s, and so as far as experts were concerned, this was just another case of a dead woolly in your back forty.

According to the Wisconsin Historical Society, "Although the museum had no plans to display the items, they knew they were important and kept them in their collections for future research."

The mammoth bone found in Frank Schaefer's soybean field didn't see the light of day for twenty-five years. Then in 1990, a museum volunteer named Dave Wasion saw something unusual in the bone and notified museum curator Dan Joyce.

The bones had cut marks from butchering.

Thirteen thousand years ago, somebody apparently had one heck of a barbecue. It was a time frame that called into question the accepted date of human arrival in North America.

Until the Kenosha discovery, the oldest site of human habitation was in Clovis, New Mexico, and dated back 11,500 years. The best archaeological minds in the business scoffed at the possibility that humans lived here any earlier. For decades, textbooks had maintained that it was Clovis first, Clovis last, and Clovis only.

Museum curator Joyce led an archaeological dig at the Schaefer farm to find more evidence. Working from Phil Sander's sketch map made in 1964, the researchers were disappointed to come up empty.

Oops. Frank Schaefer had moved one of his fenceposts.

Recalculating from the distance of the original fencepost, the mammoth's remains were rediscovered. It was a butchering site indeed, littered with evidence of Paleo-Indian activity.

During the dig at the Schaefer farm, a neighbor named John Hebior wandered over to say that he had found some bones too. Another dig was started. Another mammoth was unearthed. This one turned out to be the most complete mammoth found in North America, and it had been butchered just like the first one.

The findings were as controversial as they were exciting.

If the Kenosha dig was accurate, the story of humans in North America would have to be rewritten. The timeline of the Clovis-First theory would be seriously challenged. Some scientists scoffed. There was no way that Wisconsin had human sites older than those in New Mexico. Why and how would people live in a glaciated land?

Even a few miles up the road at the University of Wisconsin-Milwaukee, an archaeologist dismissed the notion of pre-Clovis sites in the area as nothing more than mammoth dung. The folks across town at Marquette University disagreed, and that pretty much typified the debate breaking out in the world of anthropology and archaeology.

In 1999, David Overstreet, the director of Marquette University's archaeological research center, presented his findings at a conference in Clovis, New Mexico. Talk about entering the belly of the woolly beast.

Some folks were receptive to the new findings. Others refused to consider it.

It was off to the lab for tests. The bones, too. Carbon dating finally confirmed that the two Kenosha digs were the oldest known human sites in North America—12,500 years old, thus predating the New Mexico site by one thousand years.

"We are helping to rewrite the history of the way the whole New World was populated," Joyce told the media when the findings were announced. The evidence showed that people were living in an "ice marginal" environment near glaciers and were well adapted for survival. In addition to the butchered bones, spear points capable of felling the seven-ton mammoths were found at the sites, demonstrating that the local inhabitants were clever and resourceful people.

Recent findings pushed the envelope even further. According to Overstreet, evidence has been found all over Wisconsin that people were living here up to fourteen thousand years ago, the inhabitants moving back and forth with the advance and decline of the glaciers.

Overstreet told the *Milwaukee Journal Sentinel* in 2003 that the ancient people "developed sophisticated scavenging, hunting, and boat-building strategies" in order to live here. The reason they bothered living in a climate marked by flooding, drought, and freezing? The vegetation created along the glacial margins was a buffet for mammoths—and mammoths were a smorgasbord for hunters.

"Their movements mimic the movement of their prey," Overstreet said.

Sites in Door County and near Lake Winnebago have turned up tools that could be between thirteen and fourteen thousand years old.

In 2005, the Kenosha museum wondered if their prized woolly mammoth might not be a Columbian mammoth, or maybe even a cross between a Columbian mammoth and a Jefferson mammoth.

Would it make any difference? Only insofar as woolly steaks might have tasted a little different than Columbian burgers. The people having the cookout in Frank Schaefer's farm field were the same—the earliest known inhabitants of the continent.

SHATTERED

- 1970 -

IT WASN'T UNUSUAL TO HEAR CAR WHEELS PEELING OUT on the sprawling University of Wisconsin campus, so the police officer cruising
downtown Madison didn't take notice. It was 3:40 A.M. on August
24, 1970, a muggy summer night in the city by the lakes.

Notwithstanding the brief squeal of car tires, the city and its university were quiet. The water of Lake Mendota was smooth as glass,
and the state capitol dome, one of the tallest in the nation and illu-
minated by floodlights, loomed in the haze. It was on dreamy nights
like this that the campus earned its reputation as one of the most
beautiful in the world.

At 3:41 A.M., dispatch notified the police officer that a bomb
threat had just been phoned in for Sterling Hall, home of the controversial Army Math Research Center (ARMC) on campus. Bomb
threats against ARMC had become routine on a campus known for
its Vietnam protests, and this was probably just another prank. The
caller said the bomb would detonate in five minutes.

No sooner had the policeman clipped the handheld speaker to his dashboard than a blinding flash of light shot through downtown, followed instantly by a concussion that sent a parked car hurtling across University Avenue in front of him. After gaining control of his own vehicle, the officer swung onto Charter Street.

A mushroom cloud rose above the city. Glass shards and pieces of shattered brick rained down from the sky.

Sterling Hall, all six stories of its neoclassic brick frame, was engulfed in flames.

"In the beginning," wrote Tom Bates in *RADS,* a book about the Sterling Hall bombing, "the peace movement in Madison had been broad based and non-violent, with a significant component of experienced adults."

But then came Karl Armstrong.

On New Year's Eve in 1970, Karl Armstrong and his brother Dwight had stolen a small airplane (Dwight had taken some flying lessons) and flown to Sauk City, where Karl dropped Molotov cocktails on the Badger ammunition manufacturing plant. None of the bombs caused any damage, but the "winter offensive" by the self-dubbed "New Year's Gang" emboldened Armstrong. By summer he had recruited two acquaintances, David Fine and Leo Burt, into a group he was calling, "Vanguard of the Revolution."

They set their sights on "Army Math," the U.S. Department of Defense offices located on Sterling Hall's third floor.

Meeting at a corner bar called the Nitty Gritty, Karl Armstrong and the others finalized plans to bomb Army Math using a highly explosive but commonly used material called ANFO. Typically employed by farmers to remove tree stumps, ANFO was a cheap and simple mix of ammonium nitrate and fuel oil detonated by blasting caps or dynamite.

With the proceeds from a marijuana deal, Armstrong bought forty-five gallons of fuel oil and 1,700 pounds of ammonium nitrate. Total cost: $56.12. The group filled a dozen fifty-five-gallon drums and rented a U-Haul to carry the material to a staging area outside of town.

Karl Armstrong and Leo Burt drafted a statement about the bombing. Their language was sprinkled with phrases like "revolutionary cadres" and "amerikan military genocide." In the middle of the night on August 24, the four men loaded the barrels into a stolen van, drove downtown, and wheeled into a loading bay next to Sterling Hall. Lights were on inside the building—something they had not anticipated. On the door of the Physics Department, where rocks intended for Army Math had often broken windows, somebody had placed a sign: THE STUDENTS AND FACULTY OF THE PHYSICS DEPARTMENT DEPLORE THE USE OF VIOLENCE IN THE NAME OF PEACE.

David Fine made a warning call to police when the fuse was lit.

It was too little, too late.

The explosion woke people thirty miles away. The force of it shook the perpetrators' own getaway car, even though it was blocks away. The blast took the life of Robert Fassnacht, a physics researcher who, like the perpetrators of the bombing, opposed the war in Vietnam. It caused six million dollars in damage—thirty million in today's dollars. At least twenty-six campus buildings suffered damage, University Hospital included, as well as many off-campus structures—homes, businesses, and churches. It would take thirty-eight thousand square feet of plywood just to cover all the broken windows.

Inside Sterling Hall, decades of important research in areas such as nuclear physics and superconductivity were obliterated. A major cancer project was also gone.

Army Math survived.

Listening to the radio as they made their way to Devil's Lake State Park, the bombers were dismayed to hear that they had taken the life of Doctor Fassnacht.

The group headed for the East Coast, resigned to a life underground, then split up in Toledo.

The FBI zeroed in on Armstrong's ANFO purchase and the U-Haul rental. Within days the four suspects were charged with sabotage, conspiracy, and destruction of government property, and placed on the nation's Most Wanted list. The state issued a murder charge. The University of Wisconsin Board of Regents offered a one hundred thousand dollar bounty. A nationwide dragnet began.

The bombing was denounced across the board. The mainstream antiwar movement—nonviolent and working to sway middle America—suffered guilt by association. Even those in the radical underground movement didn't want anything to do with the perpetrators.

The era of "the Sixties" had ended at approximately 3:42 A.M., August 24, 1970. The address was 475 North Chandler Street, Madison.

Author James Michener, who studied the Kent State tragedy for a 1971 book, told Karl Armstrong years later that it was Sterling Hall, not Kent State, that had punctuated the decade.

The Armstrong brothers were arrested in Canada in 1972. Fine was apprehended in California in 1976. Leo Burt was never found. In 1980 Karl Armstrong was paroled.

Sterling Hall would stand as the nation's worst act of domestic terrorism until 1995, when a bomb made of ANFO destroyed Oklahoma City's federal building.

WHERE EVERY DAY IS EARTH DAY

- 1970 -

HIGHWAY 22 RUNS THROUGH THE HEART OF WISCONSIN, from Columbia and Marquette counties in the south, through Waushara County,
then north through Shawano and Oconto counties in the northeast.
In Columbia County near Poynette, you'll find a natural overlook
with a sweeping view to the west. The pristine view of nature before
you exists mostly intact in large part due to the efforts of the people
of Wisconsin, men and women who helped elevate the environment
into the world's consciousness.

For Gaylord Nelson, state governor and United States senator
from Wisconsin, it took years of advocacy. Concerned for the environment, Nelson had an idea that President Kennedy should take a
"conservation tour" of several states. It took place in September of
1963. "For many reasons," Nelson later said, "the tour did not succeed in putting the issue onto the national political agenda." The
seed of the idea, however, was never abandoned.

In his first speech on the Senate floor—the speech every new senator uses to define the focus of their public service—he warned of the

declining condition of the nation's air and water quality. He later spoke to countless groups across the country, decrying the fact that neither candidate in the 1968 presidential campaign bothered to give a speech dedicated to the environment. "The nation's environmental issue simply was not to be found on the nation's political agenda. The people were concerned, but the politicians were not."

Nelson, who hailed from Clear Lake, continued to sound the alarm. The previous forty years had witnessed an epic economic boom—but it had come at a price. The 1960s were a time "when the darkening cloud of pollution seriously began degrading the thin envelope of air surrounding the globe; when pesticides and unrestricted waste disposal threatened the productivity of all the oceans of the world; when virtually every lake, river, and watershed in America began to show the distressing symptoms of being overloaded with polluted materials."

Nelson engaged on a speaking tour along the West Coast in 1969 and took time to view the Santa Barbara oil spill, a major environmental disaster. On the flight home, he read a magazine article about teach-ins against the Vietnam War.

"I suddenly said to myself, 'Why not have a nationwide teach-in on the environment . . .' I was satisfied that if we could tap into environmental concerns of the general public and infuse the student antiwar energy into the environmental cause, we could generate a demonstration that would force the issue onto the political agenda. It was a big gamble, but worth a try."

Turned out, the time had come. The issue Nelson had been championing alone became the cause. When he announced that a nationwide grassroots demonstration would take place on April 22, 1970, "the response was electric."

An estimated twenty million people were on hand to mark the event. Forty-two states passed Earth Day resolutions to commemorate the day. Earth Day has since become an annual worldwide event with participation from world leaders and citizens, activists and celebrities alike.

Not that there wasn't resistance. Nelson was delivering an Earth Day address at University of Wisconsin–Stevens Point when a local man stood up and yelled, "Why are you honoring the birth of Lenin?"

Seems a group of conspiracy theorists had been whispering that Earth Day was a cover for celebrating the hundredth anniversary of Vladimir Lenin's birth.

Nelson responded that there were only 365 days in a year, and about ten million people had been born on that day, including "the world's first environmentalist, St. Francis of Assisi." He added, "So was my Aunt Tillie."

Because of the wide-ranging impact of Earth Day and his legislative efforts to protect the environment, Senator Gaylord Nelson came to be ranked as one of the most significant people of the twentieth century in Wisconsin. He was awarded the Presidential Medal of Freedom, the nation's highest civilian award, on the twenty-fifth anniversary of Earth Day in 1995.

As a boy Nelson had canoed and camped along the Namekagon River in northwest Wisconsin. It was in the heart of the North Woods that he gained an appreciation for the natural world. Later, at the University of Wisconsin, he was deeply influenced by a student who had preceded him. "Everybody needs beauty as well as bread," naturalist John Muir, founder of the Sierra Club, had said, "places to play in and places to pray in, where nature may heal and cheer, and give strength to body and soul alike."

When Muir traveled between his home in Marquette County and the university, he often paused to admire the scenery from the road that is now Highway 22. This overlook in Columbia County is today called the John Muir View, the place where the young man looked to the west and saw much more than meets the eye.

It was a page right out of Muir's book when Gaylord Nelson encouraged the Kennedy administration to make a conservation tour in 1963, planting the seed that would soon grow into Earth Day.

THE (USUALLY) UNTOLD STORY OF
DAN DEVINE'S DOG

- 1974 -

THE OCTOBER 9, 1974, ISSUE OF *Time* magazine landed with all the subtlety of a hydrogen bomb. An article entitled "Haunted in Green Bay" was based on an exclusive interview with the head coach of the Green Bay Packers, Dan Devine. In these pages he described the treatment he and his family had received from the Wisconsin community.

"In the four years since he abandoned a distinguished career at the University of Missouri to join the Packers," the article read, "Devine has been the target of physical threats, personal insults and professional criticism. He has been sabotaged by his assistants, undermined by owners, and harassed by hostile fans, who have literally pursued him to his front door."

Devine had decided privately to quit the Packers coaching job at the end of the 1974 season. He was determined to take his shots at Green Bay before he left town or was fired, whichever came first. Devine unloaded his sob story to the *Time* reporter. The treatment he and his family had received was "vulgar, malicious and ugly," he said. "It makes me sick."

"Early one morning two years ago," the article read, "the Devines were awakened by a sharp bang: one of their dogs had been shot outside the house."

That little seed of a story grew into one of the all-time infamous stories in professional sports. Fans had become so obsessed with winning that they had killed the coach's dog. And this wasn't barstool hearsay printed in a third-rate publication. This came from the coach himself as told to *Time*.

The rumors in Green Bay maintained that a farmer had taken matters into his own hands after the dog had repeatedly attacked the farmer's chickens. And Devine had said that the shooting had occurred two years prior, when the Packers were enjoying their first successful season since the 1967 Super Bowl run and everything was hunky-dory in Titletown. Fans actually sported bumper stickers proclaiming, THE PACK IS DEVINE.

No matter. The magazine reporter took Devine at his word and ran with it.

Prior to Devine's hiring, only a few years had passed since the Packers' victory in Super Bowl II. It may as well have been a century. Vince Lombardi was gone, and by the end of 1970, the Packers were in the cellar of the NFL Central Division.

The team's board of directors began looking for a new coach, focusing its search on the college ranks. The executive committee chose Devine, who had amassed an impressive record in thirteen seasons with Missouri, but the decision was not unanimous. The split vote foreshadowed the dissent that would eventually wrack the organization from top to bottom.

It did not help that Devine, in his first meeting with the team, showed University of Missouri highlight films. Some of the veterans were offended from the start. "He'd tell us that the Green Bay sweep was really his play and Vince Lombardi got it from him," hall of fame safety Willie Wood told the *Milwaukee Journal Sentinel* in a 2000 interview. "That's the kind of things he'd say."

Devine's first season was a struggle. The Packers finished 4–8–2. Things were looking decidedly better, at least on the surface, in 1972, as Devine led his modestly talented team to a 10–4 record and the Central Division title. Devine was named NFC Coach of the Year. The team was hot going into the playoffs. The Pack was Devine.

But something went haywire during the playoff game against the Washington Redskins, and the Packers promising season ended with a 16–3 loss. "We just got beat by a better team," Devine explained.

His players recalled a different scenario.

"We just got outcoached," cornerback Ken Ellis told reporter Jerry Poling for the book *Downfield! The Untold Stories of the Green Bay Packers.*

By several accounts, Devine refused to make adjustments during the game and began overruling assistant coach Bart Starr's play calling.

The next season began where 1972 crash-landed, and the Packers limped to a losing record. The board of directors, coaches, and players began taking sides. One player circulated a locker room petition in support of Devine. Others ignored coaching calls made during games.

Devine decided the 1974 season would be his last in Green Bay, a decision made fairly obvious by his remarks in the *Time* article. Less than a month later, another bombshell landed when Devine mortgaged the future of the team by trading a slew of top-draft picks for aging quarterback John Hadl. (It's now considered one of the worst trades in NFL history.)

The ugly 1974 season came to an end, the Packers finishing 6–8. Devine had secretly accepted a college coaching position.

First, he submitted his resignation and negotiated a buyout on the final year of his contract. Devine then relished telling the Packers that they had been duped. "By the way," he said, moments after consummating the buyout, "I'm going to be the next head coach at Notre Dame."

On that note, Dan Devine left Green Bay.

The dog story stuck around.

When Devine died in 2002, the old hound returned with a vengeance. The Associated Press and CBS Sports reported that disgruntled Packer fans had killed Devine's dog. "Despite becoming the NFL coach of the year in 1972," read the obituary on CBS Sportsline, "Devine only lasted four seasons. During that time, some weirdo(s) shot his dog when the Packers were struggling."

The national stories may have been based on the *Time* article, or the reporters may have recycled the legend without checking the facts. Either way, the dog story was given a new lease on life. Today any number of sports Web sites containing biographical information about Devine mention that his dog was slain by disgruntled fans.

In the end, Devine came clean, sort of.

"Rumors circulated that some disgruntled fans or anti-Devine people had shot my dog," Devine said in his autobiography, published in 2000. "I honestly don't believe that was what happened."

"The dog wandered over to a nearby farm and began chasing the farmer's ducks. The farmer, a neighbor who we knew very well, fired a gun at the dog, intending to scare him and get him away from his ducks. Well, the bullet happened to hit the dog and killed him. He had every right to shoot at the dog, and he knew it and I knew it.

"Still, he felt terrible about what happened. I saw him walking toward our house, carrying the dead dog in his arms, crying uncontrollably. He kept saying, 'I didn't mean to kill him,' and I knew that was true. Still more rumors spread, even though it was a total accident, and that night I was down at his house, playing basketball with his kids."

There it is, Dan Devine demonstrating a remarkable capacity for speaking out of both sides of his mouth. He personally gave the dog story to *Time* as evidence of poor treatment in Green Bay, and he let the tall tale metastasize for years, permanently besmirching the city's reputation.

In the end Devine set the record straight, admitting that the death of his dog probably didn't have anything to do with disgruntled fans, but by then the damage was done. His obituary affirmed the old adage: When legend becomes fact, the legend usually gets printed.

THE POSSE RODE IN WISCONSIN

- 1974 -

ON AUGUST 16, 1974, INTERNAL REVENUE SERVICE Agent Fred Chicken knocked on the door of a Wisconsin farmhouse near Abbotsford. He was there for a scheduled meeting regarding the owner's taxes. Inside the house, he acknowledged three women cutting sewing patterns at the kitchen table, then followed his host Alan Grewe into the living room to review the farmer's tax records.

Things were getting tough for farmers. Tax problems were escalating with hard times along the rural landscape. It would be a meeting, the agent anticipated, like many others he had handled.

"These are some of my friends," said Grewe as the agent entered the living room. Moving instantly to surround Chicken were a roomful of men with nasty smirks and an arsenal of weapons.

It was an ambush.

Chicken turned to leave. The group's hot-tempered, 250-pound ringleader, Thomas Stockheimer, delivered a blow to the agent, sending his briefcase across the room.

"You didn't see me hit him, did you?" Stockheimer asked his colleagues. "Oh, no, not at all," the group played along.

Chicken was forced into a chair. For an hour he was interrogated and lectured about "Christian common law," world banking conspiracies involving the Rockefeller family and Jews, and parallels between Marxism and the Sixteenth Amendment (federal income taxes).

Chicken was then released without further harm.

"God bless you," Stockheimer said as the agent made his way outside into the fresh air.

A booklet thrown at Chicken during the harrowing encounter contained the platform for a racist, anti-everything group that would soon capitalize on feelings of helplessness across the impoverished rural Midwest.

The Posse Comitatus, or "the Posse" as it would become known, was about to ride.

Taking its name from the Latin "power of the county," the organization was spawned from the virulently racist Identity Church. In the early 1970s, a retired dry cleaner named Henry "Mike" Beach of Portland, Oregon, a former member of the pro-Nazi group the Silver Shirts, lifted the tenets of the Identity Church and began organizing members into the "Sheriff's Posse Comitatus." Roughly eighty cells were operating nationwide by the mid-1970s.

At the same time, America's farmers were plunged into a devastating crisis. The government had urged farmers to expand their operations, which resulted in lower prices for their products. Then the farmers were slammed with high interest rates. Banks began calling in loans, and farm after farm went belly up.

Desperate farmers began listening to the antigovernment drumbeat emanating from Posse cells in places like Kansas, Nebraska, and North Dakota. The most visible and active branch was in Wisconsin.

One month after the assault on the IRS agent in 1974, violence erupted at a Department of Natural Resources meeting in Eau Claire and Stockheimer sprayed mace at a police officer. In October a national Posse convention was held in Milwaukee. Upward of three hundred people attended, including Mike Beach. Posse chapters started in Chippewa, Manitowoc, Marathon, Shawano, and Taylor counties.

Seventeen pro-Posse candidates ran for state assembly seats on the American Party ticket in 1974. The party fielded candidates in five of nine congressional races. Posse stalwarts, though coming nowhere close to getting elected, did markedly better in counties where their chapters were located.

But it was the emergence of another Posse leader that took the organization to new heights (lows?). James Wickstrom was a traveling salesman for a tool manufacturer when he met Stockheimer. Wickstrom and others eventually set up a compound of trailers on 570 acres in Tigerton Dells, Shawano County. When one of Wickstrom's pals lost the liquor license for his local bar, Wickstrom fancied himself a municipal judge and granted a new license.

A few years later Wickstrom was the Posse's self-appointed "national director of counterinsurgency," energizing the development of the modern, government-hating, Nazi-loving, race-baiting, weapons-toting, conspiracy-embracing militia movement.

The media-savvy Wickstrom was featured in major newspaper, radio, and television programs at home and overseas. In his mainstream media appearances, the crafty Wickstrom targeted financially strapped farmers and rural residents with a watered-down, populist, antigovernment message.

Posse ranks grew. Wickstrom organized paramilitary exercises facilitated by disillusioned former military men.

Wisconsin Posse members ran for various state and federal offices on the Constitution Party ticket with Wickstrom as standard-bearer. He earned sixteen thousand votes in his 1980 United States Senate bid. Small numbers election-wise, but a battalion nutter-wise.

Then the Posse named its trailer park kingdom the "Constitutional Township of Tigerton Dells." It would be Wickstrom's downfall. As the leader of the bogus municipality, he was impersonating a public official.

Authorities made their move, and the "township" was destroyed in a 1985 raid. Officials uncovered buried guns, bomb-making equipment, and seventy thousand rounds of ammunition.

Wickstrom served more than thirteen months in jail. He was later sentenced to another thirty-eight months for counterfeiting.

Wickstrom has kept a low profile in the years since, but you could say he is attempting a comeback. He lives in Michigan's Upper Peninsula and was named national chaplain for the neo-Nazi Aryan Nation in 2004. He has hardly mellowed, rallying young skinheads to rid the nation of Jews, blacks, and Catholics.

Posse descendants are also likely to be found practicing "paper terrorism," in which illegitimate liens are filed to harass authorities and private citizens. Others have been prosecuted for filing bogus writs of habeas corpus, criminal complaints, and civil summonses, or by acting as administrative law judges and filing "Administrative Judgments."

It's not the same as paramilitary training and bomb-making in the local farm field, but the hate-filled terrorist tactics of the Posse Comitatus continue to live on, even if the organization itself is dead.

In 1993 Terry Nichols attempted to use a "Certified Fractional Reserve Check" to pay off seventeen thousand dollars in debts to the Chase Manhattan Bank. He had obtained the bogus money order from a group in Tigerton led by Thomas Stockheimer. Nichols, of course, was partner to Tim McVeigh in the Oklahoma City bombing of 1995, which took the lives of 168 men, women, and children.

THE LEGEND LIVES ON
FOR THE MIGHTY FITZ

- 1975 -

NOVEMBER 9, 1975, WAS AN UNSEASONABLY SUNNY DAY in the lakeside city of Superior, Wisconsin. Knowing that winter could settle in sooner rather than later, residents savored the fine day. A group of locals stood watching from the shore as the freighter SS *Edmund Fitzgerald* sailed from Burlington Northern ore dock #1 through the Wisconsin Point canal and into the long, calm horizon for its final run of the season.

As residents of the western terminus of the St. Lawrence Seaway (and so one of the most active shipping ports in the nation), the people of Superior were accustomed to huge Great Lakes bulk carriers coming and going from the harbor. Still, there was something about "the Fitz" that could make even the most jaded residents stop and take notice. One of the most imposing vessels ever to sail the inland sea, a veteran of 748 voyages across the lakes, and carrier of proud crew members from places like Ashland, Superior, Washburn, and

Milwaukee, the golden afternoon light almost made the ship's white trim glow.

The *Fitzgerald* was loaded with 26,100 tons of taconite pellets (processed iron ore) from Minnesota's Iron Range and bound for steel mills on the lower lakes. As he gently steered the behemoth out of the harbor, Captain Ernest McSorley, a seasoned lakes mariner, knew the good weather wasn't going to last. A storm system from the Great Plains was already bound for Lake Superior.

It's typical for storms to sweep across the lakes in November. As arctic air from Canada drops into the plains and mingles with warm air from the Gulf of Mexico, low-pressure systems ride the jet stream into the Great Lakes. November usually sees the most, and worst, storms over the lakes. The timing is especially bad in that it coincides with shippers trying to complete as many runs as possible before winter.

The *Fitzgerald* left Superior and was joined by the *Arthur M. Anderson,* another large freighter, which had departed from Two Harbors, Minnesota, under Captain Bernie Cooper. The *Fitzgerald* took the lead. The boats were seen passing Split Rock Lighthouse, Minnesota, at 4:30 P.M.

At 7:00 P.M., the National Oceanic and Atmospheric Administration (NOAA) issued a gale warning for Lake Superior, forecasting sustained winds between thirty-nine and forty-six miles per hour that night.

The warnings were upgraded in the early morning darkness of November 10. Conditions were bad, with winds gusting to fifty-seven miles per hour and waves cresting at twelve to sixteen feet; but it was nothing the crews hadn't seen before.

Through radio contact the two captains agreed to take a northerly course where they would be protected by the Canadian shore.

At dawn the storm hit Lake Superior with its full fury. The wind changed directions, pounding the freighters as they turned from Canada and headed southeast toward Whitefish Point, Michigan.

The *Anderson* tracked the *Fitzgerald* passing close to Michipi-coten and Caribou islands. "Closer than I want the *Anderson* to be," Captain Cooper told his first mate.

At 3:30 P.M., the *Fitzgerald*'s captain, McSorley, radioed Cooper. "I have a fence rail down, two vents lost or damaged, and a list. I'm checking down," he reported, indicating that he would slow to allow the *Arthur Anderson* to close the distance. The *Fitzgerald* also reported that it had two pumps working, but the situation was under control.

Two hours later winds were gusting to ninety miles per hour and the waves were at eighteen to twenty-five feet, some higher.

About 6:55 P.M., Captain Cooper felt the *Arthur Anderson*, all 767 feet of her, lurch forward. He spun around inside the pilothouse to see the unimaginable in the rear window. A monstrous wave had engulfed the stern of the vessel and was making its way along the deck. It slammed into the pilothouse and sent the bow into green water. The freighter was fully submerged.

"Then the *Anderson* just raised up and shook herself off of all that water—barroof—just like a big dog," Cooper later said.

"Another wave just like the first one or bigger hit us again."

The two waves rolled past the *Anderson* and on toward the *Fitzgerald.*

The seas were so high that the waves were interfering with the radar, and the *Anderson* kept losing sight of the *Fitzgerald,* both on the radar as well as with the bare eye.

The ships exchanged information at 7:10 P.M. "By the way, *Fitzgerald,* how are you making out with your problems?" asked the *Anderson*'s first mate.

"We are holding our own," responded McSorley.

"Okay, fine, I'll be talking to you later."

At 7:15 P.M., the *Anderson*'s radar lost the *Fitzgerald* again. But this time, it did not reappear.

Minutes later, when the weather started to clear a bit, the *Anderson* could spot other ships in the vicinity. The *Fitzgerald* was not among them.

Cooper radioed the Coast Guard's emergency line.

Months later, Cooper would tell the board of inquiry, "I watched those two waves head down the lake towards the *Fitzgerald,* and I think those were the two that sent him under."

After the *Arthur Anderson* reached safe harbor, the guard asked Cooper if he would consider turning the ship about and leading the search mission. Famously, he and his crew agreed to brave the storm once again, even though the prospects for survival were so grim that one of his sailors tape-recorded a last will and testament and put it in a wax-sealed jar.

The report of the Coast Guard investigation was released in 1977. It did little to bring closure.

The cause of the sinking could not be determined conclusively, the report stated, but the most likely scenario involved a loss of buoyancy resulting from flooding of the cargo hold "through ineffective hatch closures." This implicated the crew for failing to secure the hatches. The Lake Carriers Association disagreed strongly and appealed to the National Transportation Safety Board (NTSB). The NTSB investigation discovered "that a number of competent Great Lakes bulk cargo vessels do not maintain weathertight hatches" as they should, and concurred with the original findings—but with a dissenting opinion.

At the heart of the controversy was Captain Cooper's testimony that the *Fitzgerald* had passed too closely to Caribou Island. The dissenting opinion offered that "shoaling," or the striking of shoals, while not apparent to the captain due to the ferocity of the storm, had caused the ship to flood and list, resulting "in a total loss of buoyancy from which, diving into a wall of water, the *Fitzgerald* never recovered."

Diving expeditions made years later confirmed that the Fitzgerald had "submarined" bow first into the lake bottom, eliminating another theory that the freighter had split in two on the surface or capsized. But what caused the ship to take on water and lose enough buoyancy to be overcome when the big waves struck, sinking the mighty *Fitzgerald* in one horrific moment, will most likely remain a question for the ages.

Six thousand ships have plunged to their graves in the Great Lakes. There is only one wreck everyone knows by name.

Like the loss of the Titanic in the Atlantic Ocean, the sinking of the S.S. *Edmund Fitzgerald* in Lake Superior transcends all other disasters of its kind. As one of the largest vessels to ply the Great Lakes (the ship was longer than the lake was deep), the Milwaukee-based *Fitzgerald* was the largest lost. The entire crew of twenty-nine men was lost, leaving no survivors or eyewitnesses. The sinking happened in a violent, once-in-a-lifetime storm. And folklore, chiefly a song which made the music charts in the late '70s, is still heard today.

At the request of family members, on July 4, 1995, the *Fitzgerald*'s bronze bell was recovered. It is currently on display in the Great Lakes Shipwreck Museum in Michigan as a memorial to her lost crew.

UPON FURTHER REVIEW:
FOUR MINUTES IN TITLETOWN

- 1989 -

On a Monday morning in the fall of 1989, the world awoke to news that travel restrictions were being lifted in East Berlin. It was the beginning of the end of the Cold War.

But in Wisconsin, all the news was about a football game.

To this day local folks might not recall where they were when the Cold War ended, but you can bet your coveralls they'll remember where they were for four excruciating minutes on Sunday, November 5, 1989.

It had been five years since the Green Bay Packers had beaten their archrivals, the Chicago Bears. The team stunk, and some of the players had been involved in a variety of unsavory off-field incidents, including sexual assault. Packers fans had even suffered the indignity of watching the Bears' obese defensive lineman, "The Refrigerator," blubber his way into the end zone over a carpet of hapless, trampled Packers.

And so it went, year after year.

There was no reason to believe 1989 would be much different.

The Packer players under second-year head coach Lindy Infante were virtually anonymous. By November they had a mediocre 4–4 record, yet the Pack was showing some flare. Their victories had gone down to the wire, won by a swashbuckling, mullet-wearing quarterback with a last name that most people couldn't pronounce: Don Majkowski. Thanks to his late-game heroics and his challenging name, folks began calling him "Majik" for short.

The Pack had lost eight straight games against Chicago, the longest losing streak in their rivalry, dating back to 1921. More than 85 percent of the 1989 roster had never won against Chicago.

The local newspaper stoked the fire. "Despise the Bears?" asked one headline in the *Green Bay Press Gazette.* "Join the crowd."

"Good Wisconsin boys grew up hating the Chicago Bears," wrote columnist Don Langenkamp. "Good Wisconsin boys would watch their fathers watch the Packers and Bears play on television and their dads would snarl, 'I hate the Bears!'"

Spurred by Majkowski's surprising emergence and prodded by the local media, the team felt a sense of now-or-never urgency in the week leading up to the game.

"It makes me want to beat them real bad," said linebacker Tim Harris, a sentiment shared by roughly three million Wisconsin residents.

It was the 145th meeting between the teams. Kick-off was at noon. Temperatures were in the fifties. Attendance was 56,556.

It was clear from the start that this would be a slugfest. On the first play, Bears defensive end Richard Dent delivered an elbow into Ken Reuttgers' face, payback for a broken leg Dent had suffered the year before. Packers safety Mark Murphy soon left the game with a concussion after colliding with Matt Suhey on a pass play. The crowd was on its feet. During an early Bears possession, quarterback Jim Harbaugh pleaded with an official to stop the clock because his players couldn't hear the signals. The ref refused, and Harbaugh was forced to burn a timeout, sending the noise to even greater decibels.

The Pack came out hot, and Majkowski was at his improvisational best, moving out of the pocket to keep plays alive. At halftime the Packers held a seven-to-three advantage.

In the third quarter, Bears quarterback Jim Harbaugh took a blow to the head from Packers defensive back Robert Brown. Bears surrounded Brown, pushing and cursing the Packer.

The Bears kicked a thirty-seven-yard field goal, then took a thirteen-to-seven lead with an eighty-yard touchdown drive late in the third quarter.

Suddenly the tide had turned—like it always seemed to do against the Pack. The tension in the stadium was as thick as the overcast sky.

The game entered the fourth quarter. The fans stood screaming and clutching their beer cups.

Twice the Packers were mere yards away from scoring. The first time Majkowski lost the ball at the Bears' ten-yard line when he was slammed by the unrelenting Chicago defense. The second time he was intercepted at the ten.

Infante collared his quarterback on the sideline. "Don't worry. Keep your head up. You're still going to be the hero of this game."

But only if the Packers got the ball back.

The defense, which ranked second to last in the league for yards allowed, twice stopped the Bears down the stretch. They were helped by a penalty that nullified a critical third-down conversion for the Bears, a call head coach Mike Ditka would later single out as poor officiating.

When the Packers started a drive from their own twenty-seven-yard line, there were only four minutes remaining.

They did it the hard way. At one point, the Bears should have made an interception on a tipped pass—but Packers tight end Ed West wrestled the ball away.

Little more than a minute remained when Majkowski again had the ball knocked out of his hands. The live ball lay untouched for several seconds—an eternity—before Packers center Blair Bush fell on it. Another bullet dodged.

It was fourth-and-one at the Bears' ten-yard line. Do or die time.

Rookie running back Vince Workman, on his first professional play, dove three yards for the first down. But then first-and-goal at the seven-yard line became fourth down at the fourteen. The team was moving backward.

Forty-one seconds remained. Majkowski would have to pull another desperate play out of thin air. Twice before he had lost the ball in scoring position.

Do or die *again,* this time for the game.

On the next play Majkowski dropped back to pass. The Bears came hard. Majkowski escaped the pocket, his mullet flying. Trace Armstrong gave chase toward the Packer sideline. Majkowski could hear the 260-pound man behind him. The quarterback started to bring his arm forward, resigned to throwing the pass up for grabs and hoping for the best, when Sterling Sharpe entered the corner of his eye moving left to right. Majkowski cocked his arm, bought another second, and drilled a pass off balance.

Sharpe caught the ball in a den of astonished Bear defenders. Touchdown.

The Packers' bench, the stadium, and living rooms across the state erupted.

Then, an eerie silence fell. An official had thrown a penalty flag, ruling that Majkowski had stepped over the line of scrimmage as he threw the touchdown. The Bears offense hustled onto the field to execute a play and run out the clock.

But wait.

The officials, in their first season using replay as a device to double-check close calls, called a timeout to review the play.

For four long minutes players milled around the field anxiously, fans stood frozen in place, millions of viewers clung to their television sets. It was an unprecedented amount of time to review a play.

The head referee finally walked to the middle of the field, flipped the switch on his microphone, and turned to the crowd.

"Upon further review, we have a reversal . . . "

Whatever was said after that was inaudible. Lambeau Field's concrete and steel foundation shook under the celebration.

"For that to happen at the end of the game, it made me sick," said one Chicago Bear.

"This is a bad way to lose a game, especially against the Packers," Jim Harbaugh said.

"I'm overwhelmed with emotion," said Packer Brian Noble. "Guys were crying. Guys were screaming. We've been through some games with these guys that have come down to the wire like this one did. Somehow, we always found ourselves on the short end of the stick. I guarantee you right now, there's a party in Green Bay tonight."

"So, set 'em up bartender," wrote one columnist. "Tonight we toast the Green Bay Packers."

The toasts never really stopped. In 2005, Don "Majik" Majkowski was inducted into the Green Bay Packer Hall of Fame, if for no other reason than winning the Instant Replay Game on a glorious November afternoon.

THE SUPERNOVA OF DEPRAVITY

- 1991 -

JUST BEFORE 2:00 A.M. ON MAY 27, 1991, Milwaukee police received a 911 call. A naked and disoriented young man had been seen at the corner of Twenty-fifth and State. Paramedics arrived on the scene and wrapped the youth in a blanket. Two police officers arrived moments later, as did Jeffrey Dahmer, a fair-haired resident of a nearby apartment complex.

Dahmer explained calmly that this was his nineteen-year-old boyfriend. They had been drinking and had gotten into an argument. His boyfriend was so drunk that he had stormed out of the apartment without any clothes on.

The police bought the story, despite protests from bystanders who had gathered on the corner. City cops had seen stranger stuff than this. They allowed Dahmer to take the young Laotian, Konerak Sinthasomphone, back to his apartment.

In truth, Sinthasomphone was fourteen, he had been drugged, and within moments after returning to the apartment, he was dead.

The close call only accelerated Dahmer's demented ways. By summer he was killing a person a week.

On July 22, Dahmer lured another man into his home. The would-be victim managed to escape when Dahmer tried to handcuff him. With the cuffs dangling from one hand, the naked man flagged down a police car.

"The devil," the man told officers, was going to cut out his heart and eat it. The story was so bizarre it took some convincing, but police decided to follow up and knocked on room 213 of the Oxford Apartments.

After investigating the apartment, the police took Jeffrey Dahmer into custody and charged him with seventeen murders dating back to 1978.

Forensic experts found the remains of eleven victims in his apartment. Torture, necrophilia, cannibalism . . . Jeffrey Dahmer made Wisconsin's previously most famous ghoul, Ed Gein, seem like a model of discretion. As Richard Hendricks and Linda Godfrey said in their book *Weird Wisconsin,* "In 1991, Ed Gein was totally eclipsed by Jeffrey Dahmer, a hot new nova of depravity unlike anything ever seen before."

Lucky us.

Dahmer put up token resistance when officers handcuffed him that sweltering July night, but in little time he threw in the towel and began cooperating fully, matter-of-factly explaining all the unimaginable, macabre details of how he tortured and ate his victims. He eventually pled guilty by reason of insanity. The jury, however, found him sane. As the trial concluded, he read a four-page apology to the court:

> *It is now over. This has never been a case of trying to*
> *get free. I didn't ever want freedom. Frankly, I wanted*

*death for myself. This was a case to tell the world that
I did what I did, but not for reasons of hate. I hated
no one. I knew I was sick or evil or both. Now I
believe I was sick. The doctors have told me about my
sickness, and now I have some peace. I know how
much harm I have caused . . . Thank God there will
be no more harm that I can do. I believe that only the
Lord Jesus Christ can save me from my sins . . . I ask
for no consideration.*

He was sentenced to fifteen consecutive life terms plus fifty-seven years and sent to Columbia County Correctional Institute in Portage.

Like the folks in Plainfield who burned Ed Gein's house before it became a tourist attraction, the powers that be in Milwaukee moved quickly to cleanse itself of the stain named Dahmer. The Oxford Apartment complex was demolished in 1992. His possessions, however, were scheduled to go on auction. Again Milwaukee stepped in, raising enough private-sector money to buy the items and have them destroyed.

By the time Dahmer was killed by another inmate in 1994, he left nothing behind but his remains.

Even that proved more than enough.

"The secret is out," reported the *Wisconsin State Journal.* "Jeffrey Dahmer's body is being kept in a freezer in the basement of Dane County's Public Safety Building on Doty Street and his brain is in a jar at the offices of the state pathologist on the UW–Madison campus."

Dahmer had requested cremation, and that would come eventually, but his remains, er, remained as evidence in the trial of the inmate who had bludgeoned him to death with a weightlifting bar.

Then, as if from a bad horror movie—a really bad movie—came *The Return of Dahmer's Brain!*

That's right. After Dahmer's body had been cremated, his brain remained on a shelf at the University of Wisconsin. Why? Dahmer's parents were divorced and they disagreed on what to do with it. His father wanted the brain cremated and the whole sordid story brought to an end, while his mother wanted it released to Georgetown University for study.

A hearing was held in Columbia County Circuit Court. Dahmer's father participated by phone, his mother's attorney appeared in the courtroom, and the brain stayed at the University of Wisconsin.

Judge Daniel George was not convinced of the scientific benefits of releasing the brain. "I think the closure aspect of it—bringing this chapter to a conclusion without perpetuating more gruesome, ghoulish kinds of interest—was more beneficial for the victims, community, and families," he said.

After the court decision, a reporter visited the local library for reaction.

"Of course, everyone immediately started comparing [Dahmer] with Ed Gein," volunteered one staff member, who noted that the library's materials about the serial killers were so popular that they were either worn out or had turned up missing.

"I think [people are] always fascinated by murders, and the more bizarre, the better."

It doesn't get more bizarre than Jeffrey Dahmer, and like Ed Gein, he's Wisconsin's forever, whether we want him or not.

WISCONSIN FACTS & TRIVIA

Wisconsin became the thirtieth state in the union on May 28, 1848.

Pepin County was the birthplace of Laura Ingalls Wilder, author of the "Little House" books. A replica of her log cabin is located in Pepin, Wisconsin.

Architect Frank Lloyd Wright was born on June 8, 1867, near Richland Center in Richland County. Spring Green in Iowa County is home to Frank Lloyd Wright's estate, Taliesin, which served as his residence and workshop for forty-eight years.

Wisconsin's oldest community, Green Bay, has been under the reign of three nations in its history: France, Britain, and the United States.

The dome of Wisconsin's state capitol building is modeled after the nation's capitol in Washington, D.C., but it was constructed a few inches shorter than the federal building.

Wisconsin has 15,057 lakes covering a total of 1,439 square miles. The state fish, the muskellunge, can be found in more than seven hundred of these lakes.

Every year, more than 1.3 million Wisconsin fishing licenses are sold and more than 61 million fish are caught.

The University of Wisconsin football team, the Badgers, is the only Big Ten team to win back-to-back Rose Bowls (1999 & 2000).

The International Snowmobile Racing Hall of Fame is located in St. Germain. The World Championship Snowmobile Derby is held annually in Eagle River.

Milwaukee's Summerfest is the world's biggest outdoor music festival, drawing nearly one million visitors per year.

Known as America's Dairyland, Wisconsin is home to more than 1.3 million dairy cows, which annually produce milk for roughly 42 million people, butter for 68 million, and cheese for 86 million.

Wisconsin is bordered by two Great Lakes, Michigan and Superior, as well as the Mississippi River.

At 165 feet, Big Manitou Falls in Pattison State Park is Wisconsin's highest waterfall.

Wisconsin is home to Harley-Davidson, the world's largest motorcycle manufacturer.

Chalet Cheese Co-op in Monroe in the only cheese factory in the United States that still makes the strong-smelling Limburger cheese.

Wisconsin is not only the largest producer of cheese in the nation (with more than 350 varieties) but it's also the largest producer of cranberries and ginseng.

The first ice cream sundae was created in Two Rivers in 1881 at Edward Berner's ice cream parlor. At first the confection was only sold on Sundays, but it soon proved too popular for only one day of the week.

Milwaukee resident, Christopher Lathan Sholes, invented the typewriter. Today the Milwaukee Public Museum has the world's largest collection of typewriters with more than seven hundred.

Gangster Al Capone built his cottage for weekend "getaways" in Courderay. The Hideout, as it is known today, serves as a tourist attraction and supper club.

The coldest temperature ever recorded in Wisconsin was minus 54 degrees on January 24, 1922, at Danbury in Burnett County.

Twenty men from the Madison area comprised the first class of students at the University of Wisconsin in 1849. Today more than forty-one thousand students attend the UW Madison campus.

Door County, the "thumb" of Wisconsin that juts into Lake Michigan, is home to more miles of coastline (250), more lighthouses (10), and more state parks (5) than any other county in the United States.

"On, Wisconsin" one of the nation's most recognizable college fight songs, was written in 1909 by William Purdy. It became the state song in 1959.

The first auto race in history took place between two steam-powered cars in 1878. It took the winner thirty-three hours to travel from Green Bay to Madison. The other car broke down.

Wisconsin was the first state to have a "workmen's compensation" law, the first to pass unemployment compensation, and the first to pass a law against discrimination of women.

In 1856, in Watertown, Margaretha Meyer Schurz opened the first kindergarten in the United States.

Wisconsin leads the nation in paper manufacturing.

The Green Bay Packers, founded in 1919, joined the American Professional Football Association in 1921 (renamed the NFL in 1922).

The team has won more world championship titles (twelve) than any other pro football team. They also have twenty-one players in the Pro Football Hall of Fame.

Hearthstone, the Appleton residence of Henry Rogers, was the world's first private residence lit by hydroelectricity.

Wisconsin was the birthplace of more than one hundred circuses. The town of Delevan alone was home base for twenty-six circuses between 1847 and 1894. Beginning in 1884, Baraboo served as the winter headquarters for the Ringling Brothers' World Greatest Shows.

The SS *Edmund Fitzgerald,* lost in a violent storm on Lake Superior in November 1975, was named for the chairman of the Northwestern Mutual Life Insurance Company in Milwaukee. The company commissioned the ship in the 1950s.

In 1910 Milwaukee voters elected Emil Seidel the nation's first socialist mayor and Victor Berger the first socialist congressman.

BIBLIOGRAPHY

Aztalan: Bones of Contention—3000 BC

Birmingham, Robert A., and Lynne G. Goldstein. *Aztalan: Mysteries of an Ancient Indian Town*. Madison: Wisconsin Historical Society Press, 2005.

Davis McBride, Sarah, ed. *History Just Ahead: A Guide to Wisconsin's Historical Markers*. Madison: State Historical Society of Wisconsin, 1999.

Kasparek, Jon, Bobbie Malone, and Erica Schock. *Wisconsin History Highlights: Delving Into the Past*. Madison: Wisconsin Historical Society Press, 2004.

Rock Lake Research Society. http://www.rocklakeresearch.com/.

Seely, Ron. "Renewed interest in the secrets of Aztalan," *Wisconsin State Journal*, January 3, 2004.

Wisconsin Department of Natural Resources. "Aztalan State Park." www.dnr.state.wi.us/ORG/LAND/parks/specific/aztalan/#museum.

Lost and Found—1634

Davis McBride, Sarah, ed. *History Just Ahead: A Guide to Wisconsin's Historical Markers*. Madison: State Historical Society of Wisconsin, 1999.

Rodesch, Jerrold. "Jean Nicolet." *Voyageur Magazine*, Spring 1984, 4–8.

Rudolph, Jack. *The Green Bay Area in History and Legend.* Green Bay: Brown County Historical Society, 2004.

Smith, Alice E. *The History of Wisconsin, Volume 1: From Exploration to Statehood.* Madison: State Historical Society of Wisconsin, 1985.

Vimont, Barthelemy. *The Journey of Jean Nicolet, 1634.* American Journeys Collection, Wisconsin Historical Society Digital Library and Archives, 2003. www.wisconsinhistory.org/. www.americanjourneys.org/aj-043/index.asp.

Passion in Prairie du Chien—1832

"Jefferson Davis in the 90s," *Milwaukee Sentinel,* November 10, 1895.

"Jefferson Davis Met and Won Daughter of Zachary Taylor at Fort Crawford," *Wisconsin State Journal,* November 25, 1923.

"Jeff Davis' Wisconsin Elopement Which Really Wasn't an Elopement," *Milwaukee Journal,* February 24, 1928.

"Zachary Taylor." www.whitehouse.gov/history/presidents/zt12 .html.

"Zachary Taylor's Daughter Wooed by Jefferson Davis At Wisconsin Frontier Outpost," *Milwaukee Sentinel,* November 4, 1923.

"Last Veteran of Civil War Dies Monday," *Shawano Leader Advocate,* April 6, 1933.

Rice University. "The Papers of Jefferson Davis." http://jefferson davis.rice.edu/.

King James Strang—1844

Holmes, Fred. *Badger Saints and Sinners.* Milwaukee: E. M. Hale and Co., 1939.

"The man who shot Strang." *Beaver Beacon Magazine,* October 2002. www.beaverbeacon.com/2002-10-October/The_Man_ who_shot_Strang.html.

Odd Wisconsin Archive, Wisconsin Historical Society, "The Crowning of King James," www.wisconsinhistory.org/odd/ archives/001561.asp.

Wisconsin Local History and Biography Article, Wisconsin Historical Society: "Saw A King Crowned," *Green Bay Advocate,* February 6, 1905.

John McCaffary's Body—1851
"Capital Punishment in Wisconsin and the Nation," April 1995, Legislative Reference Bureau Informational Bulletin 95–1, www.legis.state.wi.us.

"Execution of John McCaffrey," *Kenosha Telegraph,* May 30, 1851.

"Horrible murder," *Kenosha Democrat,* July 25, 1850.

Pendleton, Alexander T. and Blaine R. Renfert. "A Brief History of Wisconsin's Death Penalty," *Wisconsin Lawyer Magazine,* August 1, 1993.

Striking a Blow for Freedom—1854
"Helped Save Glover," *Milwaukee Sentinel,* June 10, 1900.

Holmes, Fred. *Badger Saints and Sinners.* Milwaukee: E. M. Hale and Co., 1939.

"Joshua Glover; Memorializing a brave moment." *Milwaukee Journal Sentinel,* May 12, 2006.

Kane, Eugene. "A triumph in racial justice leaves a legacy to act upon," *Milwaukee Journal Sentinel,* undated, www.jsonline.com/ story/index.aspx?id=339699.

Kasparek, Jon, Bobbie Malone, and Erica Schock. *Wisconsin History Highlights: Delving Into the Past.* Madison: Wisconsin Historical Society Press, 2004.

Legler, Henry. "Rescue of Joshua Glover, A Runaway Slave" from Leading Events of Wisconsin History. www.library.wisc.edu/ etext/WIReader/WER1124.html.

"Ripon's Booth War, 1860," Wisconsin Local History Network. www.wlhn.org/topics/boothwar/booth_war_intro.htm.

Commies, Swingers, and Republicans, Oh My!—1854
Davis McBride, Sarah, ed. *History Just Ahead: A Guide to Wisconsin's Historical Markers.* Madison: State Historical Society of Wisconsin, 1999.

"He was father of Republican Party," *Milwaukee Journal,* June 2, 1929.

Holmes, Fred. *Badger Saints and Sinners,* Milwaukee: E. M. Hale and Co., 1939.

"Milwaukee Man One of Seventeen Who Christened Republican Party," (newspaper unidentified), December 1, 1906, www .wisconsinhistory.org/turningpoints/search.asp?id=948.

Republican National Committee, www.gop.com/About.

Our Prize-Winning Dairy Air—1872
Buenker, John D. *The History of Wisconsin, Volume IV: The Progressive Era, 1893–1914.* Madison: State Historical Society of Wisconsin, 1998.

Cheese Facts and Figures, Wisconsin Milk Marketing Board, www.wisdairy/AllAboutCheese/CheeseFactsAndFigures.aspx.

Davis McBride, Sarah, ed. *History Just Ahead: A Guide to Wisconsin's Historical Markers.* Madison: State Historical Society of Wisconsin, 1999.

Hoard's Dairyman, The National Dairy Farm Magazine, www .hoards.com.

Kasparek, Jon, Bobbie Malone, and Erica Schock. *Wisconsin History Highlights: Delving Into the Past.* Madison: Wisconsin Historical Society Press, 2004.

News releases, World Cheese Championship, Madison, Wisconsin Cheese Makers Association, www.wischeesemakersassn.org/ wccc/2006/index.html.

Risjord, Norman K. *Wisconsin Magazine of History,* Spring 2005, "From the Plow to the Cow," 40–49.

Holocaust—1871

"The Great Peshtigo Fire of 1871." www.peshtigofire.info/.

Kasparek, Jon, Bobbie Malone, and Erica Schock. *Wisconsin History Highlights: Delving Into the Past.* Madison: Wisconsin Historical Society Press, 2004.

Pernin, Peter. *The Great Peshtigo Fire: An Eyewitness Account.* Madison: State Historical Society of Wisconsin, 1999.

Saturday Afternoon Daredevil—1882

Apps, Jerry. *Ringlingville USA: The Stupendous Story of Seven Siblings and Their Stunning Circus Success.* Madison: Wisconsin Historical Society Press, 2005.

Holmes, Fred. *Badger Saints and Sinners.* Milwaukee: E. M. Hale and Co., 1939.

Kasparek, Jon, Bobbie Malone, and Erica Schock. *Wisconsin History Highlights: Delving Into the Past.* Madison: Wisconsin Historical Society Press, 2004.

Fighting Bob—1904

Buenker, John D. *The History of Wisconsin, Volume IV: The Progressive Era, 1893–1914.* Madison: State Historical Society of Wisconsin, 1998.

Holmes, Fred. *Badger Saints and Sinners.* Milwaukee: E. M. Hale and Co., 1939.

Kasparek, Jon, Bobbie Malone, and Erica Schock. *Wisconsin History Highlights: Delving Into the Past.* Madison: Wisconsin Historical Society Press, 2004.

United States Congress, "La Follette, Robert Marion," http:// bioguide.congress.gov/scripts/biodisplay.pl?index=L000004.

Weisberger, Bernard A. *The La Follettes of Wisconsin.* Madison: University of Wisconsin Press, 1994.

Assassin!—1912

"Glass used by Teddy Roosevelt after assassination attempt." Wisconsin Historical Society, www.wisconsinhistory.org/museum/ artifacts/archives/001692.asp.

"The Health and Medical History of President Theodore Roosevelt," Dr. Zebra, www.doctorzebra.com/prez/g26.htm.

"This date in Wisconsin, Oct. 14, 1912," *Classic Wisconsin,* www.classicwisconsin.com/features/assassin.html.

Mayhem at Taliesin—1914

Houghton Mifflin, Wright, Frank Lloyd, www.college.hmco.com/ history/readerscomp/rcah/html/ah_094400_wrightfrankl.htm.

"Negro Murderer of Seven," *Weekly Home News,* August 20, 1914.

"Seven Killed and Two Injured by Negro at Wright Bungalow," *Dodgeville Chronicle,* August 21, 1914.

World of Wonder, www.worldofwonder.net/productions/networks/ bbc/frank_lloyd_wright_murder_myth_and_modernism.wow.

Carl's Sled—1924

Davis McBride, Sarah, ed. *History Just Ahead: A Guide to Wisconsin's Historical Markers.* Madison: State Historical Society of Wisconsin, 1999.

The Eliason Motor Toboggan, The History of Eliason Snowmobiles 1924–1963, company history.

Eliason Snowmobiles, www.eliason-snowmobile.com/.

Cool Cal Chilled in Superior—1928

"Coolidge's death recalls his visits to Madison," *Capital Times,* January 5, 1933. www.wisconsinhistory.org.

"Coolidge to Spend Vacation in Wisconsin," *Wisconsin State Journal,* May 31, 1928. www.wisconsinhistory.org.

Kasparek, Jon, Bobbie Malone, and Erica Schock. *Wisconsin History Highlights: Delving Into the Past.* Madison: Wisconsin Historical Society Press, 2004.

"1,000 Madisonians fail to see Cal," *Wisconsin State Journal,* June 13, 1928. www.wisconsinhistory.org.

"Trout and Comfort to Greet President," *Wisconsin State Journal,* June 12, 1928. www.wisconsinhistory.org.

White House, www.whitehouse.gov/history/presidents/.

The State That Made Prohibition Infamous—1929

"American Brewery History Page," www.beerhistory.com/.

"Enforcement of the Prohibition Laws: Official Records of the National Commission on Law Observance and Enforcement: A Prohibition Survey of the State of Wisconsin." www.wisconsin history.org/turningpoints/search.asp?id=1273.

"Famous Gardens and Wein Stubens Gave City its Charm in the Early Days," *Milwaukee Sentinel*, February 21 1932. www .wisconsinhistory.org.

"Schlitz Garden Enters History," *Milwaukee Journal*, March 6, 1921, www.wisconsinhistory.org.

Smith, Alice E. *The History of Wisconsin, Volume 1: From Exploration to Statehood.* Madison: State Historical Society of Wisconsin, 1985.

"When beer, Milwaukee style, was introduced to New York," *Milwaukee Journal*, May 30, 1930. www.wisconsinhistory.org.

Smiling Joe—1930

Kasparek, Jon, Bobbie Malone, and Erica Schock. *Wisconsin History Highlights: Delving Into the Past.* Madison: Wisconsin Historical Society Press, 2004.

Outagamie County Historical Society, Virtual Exhibits, www.fox valleyhistory.org/mccarthy/index.

Reeves, Thomas. *The Life and Times of Joe McCarthy.* Briarcliff Manor, New York: Stein and Day, 1982.

"The Rise and Fall of Senator Joe McCarthy: A Modern Tragedy." *Voyageur Magazine*, Summer/Fall 2005, Brown County Historical Society, 30–35.

Valley of the Molls—1934

"County Jail is Honeymoon Hotel to Gangster Girl," *Capital Times,* April 25, 1934.

"Dillinger Gang Molls Behind Bars Here," *Wisconsin State Journal,* April 24, 1934

Federal Bureau of Investigation, www.fbi.gov/libref/historic/famcases/dillinger/dillinger.

"Gangster's Bride Spends Honeymoon Alone in Cell," *Wisconsin State Journal,* April 25, 1934.

"Posse Hunts Nelson Near City," *Capital Times,* April 30, 1934.

It Happened in Necedah, Allegedly—1950

"Final Visit of The Blessed Virgin Reported Saturday," *Necedah Republican,* October 12, 1950.

McCann, Dennis. "Visits drew crowd, not credence," *Milwaukee Journal Sentinel,* April 2, 1998.

"Mrs. Van Hoof Awaits Vision," *La Crosse Tribune,* August 13, 1950.

"Mrs. Van Hoof Quotes Words Spoken Again," *La Crosse Tribune,* August 16, 1950.

"Pilgrims Gather at Necedah Shrine," *Necedah Republican,* August 17, 1950.

Queen of the Holy Rosary Mediatrix of Peace Shrine, www.necedah shrine.com/.

"Special Pilgrimage Trains To Necedah," *Necedah Republican,* August 10, 1950.

"Special Trains, Buses Ready for Necedah 'Visitation' Trip," *Necedah Republican,* July 27, 1950.

A Summer in Eau Claire—1952
Baseball Hall of Fame, www.baseballhalloffame.org.

"Roach Hurls Win; Road Trip Next," *Eau Claire Leader,* June 21, 1952.

Poling, Jerry. *A Summer Up North,* Madison: University of Wisconsin Press, 2002.

Psycho—1958
Crime Library, www.crimelibrary.com/serial_killers/notorious/gein/bill_1.html. Chapters 1–11 by Rachael Bell and Marilyn Bardsley.

"Gein's missing tombstone finally recovered in Seattle," *Associated Press,* June 21, 2001.

Hendricks, Richard, and Linda Godfrey. *Weird Wisconsin: Your Travel Guide to Wisconsin's Local Legends and Best Kept Secrets,* New York: Barnes & Noble Books, 2005.

Jones, Meg. "Crime Doesn't Pay, but Will It Sell? Plainfield property where killer Ed Gein lived is up for auction on eBay," *Milwaukee Journal Sentinel,* April 6, 2006.

"Man puts Ed Gein property up for sale," *Associated Press,* April 7, 2006.

The Making of a President's Baby—1960
Davis McBride, Sarah, ed. *History Just Ahead: A Guide to Wisconsin's Historical Markers.* Madison: State Historical Society of Wisconsin, 1999.

The Gideons International, http://www.gideons.org.

"Kennedy addresses Fieldhouse audience," *Wisconsin State Journal,* March 26, 1960.

Orwell Today, www.orwelltoday.com.

"Senator Kennedy Campaigns in Boscobel," *Boscobel Dial,* March 31, 1960.

University of Wisconsin–Stout University Foundation newsletter, Campaign Trail Through Menomonie, Winter 2004, www .uwstout.edu.

Our Woollies Changed History—1964
Jensen, Arlene. "Mammoth Bones 12,310 Years Old," *Kenosha News,* March 12, 2000.

Kasparek, Jon, Bobbie Malone, and Erica Schock. *Wisconsin History Highlights: Delving Into the Past.* Madison: Wisconsin Historical Society Press, 2004.

Rust, Susanne. "Is Mammoth Woolly? Kenosha Museum Reconsiders an Old, Old Friend," *Milwaukee Journal Sentinel,* December 18, 2005.

Shattered—1970
Bates, Tom. *RADS: The 1970 Bombing of the Army Math Research Center at the University of Wisconsin and Its Aftermath.* New York, NY: HarperCollins, 1992.

"Sterling Hall Bombing." www.madison.com/library/LEE/sterling hall.

Where Every Day Is Earth Day—1970
Anderson, Warren. "Rest in Peace Gaylord Nelson, Founder of Earth Day." Sierra Club, http://florida.sierraclub.org/northeast/ education/gaylord1.html.

Aukoffer, Frank A. "Obituary, Gaylord A. Nelson 1916–2005, Earth Day Founder Was a Voice Crying Out For the Wilderness Clear Lake Native Served as Governor, U.S. Senator," *Milwaukee Journal Sentinel,* July 4, 2005.

Davis McBride, Sarah, ed. *History Just Ahead: A Guide to Wisconsin's Historical Markers.* Madison: State Historical Society of Wisconsin, 1999.

Exhibit, Wisconsin Historical Society, 816 State St., Madison.

Kasparek, Jon, Bobbie Malone, and Erica Schock. *Wisconsin History Highlights: Delving Into the Past.* Madison: Wisconsin Historical Society Press, 2004.

National Park Service, www.nps.gov/archive/jomu/qufacts.htm.

Sierra Club, "John Muir Exhibit," www.sierraclub.org/john_muir_exhibit.

Wilderness Society, "Gaylord Nelson," www.wilderness.org/About Us/Nelson_Bio.cfm.

The (Usually) Untold Story of Dan Devine's Dog—1974
Baum, Bob. "Ex Football Coach Dan Devine Dies at 77," *Associated Press,* May 18, 2002.

Christl, Cliff. "A lasting impression—Devastating trade defined Devine's legacy with Packers," *Milwaukee Journal Sentinel,* May 10, 2002.

Devine, Dan. *Simply Devine: Memoirs of a Hall of Fame Coach.* Champaign, IL: Sports Publishing, 2000.

"Haunted in Green Bay." *Time,* October 9, 1974.

Poling, Jerry. *Downfield! The Untold Stories of the Green Bay Packers,* Madison: Prairie Oak Press, 1996.

The Posse Rode in Wisconsin—1974

Buchanon, Susy. "Return of the Pastor," Southern Poverty Law Center, www.splcenter.org.

Kasparek, Jon, Bobbie Malone, and Erica Schock. *Wisconsin History Highlights: Delving Into the Past.* Madison: Wisconsin Historical Society Press, 2004.

Levitas, Daniel. *The Terrorist Next Door: The Militia Movement and the Radical Right,* New York: Thomas Dunne Books, St. Martin's Griffin, 2002.

Low, Marsha. "Anti-Semitic Preacher Get Attention, Fear," *Detroit Free Press,* April 12, 2004.

The Legend Lives On for the Mighty Fitz—1975

"Edmund Fitzgerald." Great Lakes Shipwreck Museum, www .shipwreckmuseum.org.

Jenny, Nolan. "The fateful voyage of the Edmund Fitzgerald" *Detroit News Notable events,* undated, http://info.detnews.com/ history/story/index.cfm?id=114&category=events.

"NTSB Edmund Fitzgerald Accident Report." U.S. Coast Guard, www.uscg.mil.

Ratigan, William. *Great Lakes Shipwrecks & Survivals.* Grand Rapids, Michigan: Wm. B. Eerdmans Publishing Co, 1977.

Upon Further Review: Four Minutes in Titletown—1989

Burke, Don. "Official Says Position of Ball Was Key in Call," *Milwaukee Sentinel,* November 6, 1989.

———. "Replay Ruling Sends Packers to Victory," *Milwaukee Sentinel* November 6, 1989.

Green Bay Packers Web site, www.packers.com.

"Instant Replay Ruling Leaves Bears Bitter," *Milwaukee Sentinel* November 6, 1989.

Lea, Bud. "Majik Ad-libbed on TD," *Milwaukee Sentinel,* November 6, 1989.

———. "Majik Moment! Packers Win 1 For the Faithful, Deck Bears, 14-13," *Milwaukee Sentinel,* November 6, 1989.

McGinn, Bob. "Packers Prove Parity with Win," *Green Bay Press Gazette,* November 6, 1989.

———. "Packers' un-Bearable Streak at 8," *Green Bay Press Gazette,* November 1, 1989.

———. "Veterans: Beating Bears a Career High," *Green Bay Press Gazette,* November 6, 1989.

Mulhern, Tom. "Eye in the Sky Saves Packers," *Green Bay Press Gazette,* November 6, 1989.

———. "Finally! Packers Savor Rare Victory Over Bears" *Green Bay Press Gazette,* November 6, 1989.

———. "Majkowski Convinced Pass was Behind Line," *Green Bay Press Gazette,* November 6, 1989.

"Packers become instant heroes," *Green Bay Press Gazette,* November 6, 1989.

Vandermause, Mike. "Dikta Holds His Temper Despite Loss," *Milwaukee Sentinel,* November 6, 1989.

Walter, Tony and Paul Srubas. "'I'm in Better Mood Today,' Says One Fan – Beating Bears the Tonic," *Green Bay Press Gazette*, November 6, 1989.

The Supernova of Depravity—1991
Crime Library, www.crimelibrary.com.

"Dahmer's instruments of death to be sold," CNN & Associated Press, April 24, 1996, www-cgi.cnn.com/US/9604/24/ newsbriefs/index.html.

"Dahmer's Remains Still at Morgue," *Wisconsin State Journal*, August 2, 1995.

Hendricks, Richard, and Linda Godfrey. *Weird Wisconsin: Your Travel Guide to Wisconsin's Local Legends and Best Kept Secrets.* New York: Barnes & Noble Books, 2005.

Portage Daily Register. "Finding Jeff," "Squabble Over Dahmer's Brain," and "Dahmer's Death Brought Unwanted Media Attention to Portage," November 28, 2004.

INDEX

ABOUT THE AUTHOR

Michael Bie, a Green Bay native, is perhaps best known for his Web site, www.classicwisconsin.com. He was formally educated at UW–Stevens Point and informally educated at the Upper Wisconsin River Yacht Club, Stevens Point; Del's Bar, La Crosse; and The Joynt, Eau Claire. As a freelance writer, he has multiple magazine and newspaper credits to his name. He can usually be found pursuing an interest in all things Wisconsin. Bie even spent several summers crisscrossing the state by bicycle until he realized that motor vehicles provided the same service in a fraction of the time. Occasionally he considers taking his bike out of storage.